Bristol Central Lending Library
College Green
Bristol BS1 5TL
Tel: Renewals 903 7240
        Enquiries 903 7250

D1394039

BRISTOL CITY COUNCIL
LIBRARY SERVICES
WITHDRAWN AND OFFERED FOR SALE
SOLD AS SEEN

AN 0562135 6

EGYPTIAN ART
DRAWINGS & PAINTINGS

EGYPTIAN ART
DRAWINGS & PAINTINGS

Hannelore Kischkewitz

photographs by
Werner Forman

D 340814

Class	
No. 709 · 32	
Alloc. AA 9/89	AS
AV N COUNTY LIBRARY	

HAMLYN

Published in 1989 by
The Hamlyn Publishing Group Limited
Michelin House, 81 Fulham Road
London SW3 6RB
and distributed for them by
Octopus Distribution Services Limited
Rushden, Northamptonshire, England NN10 9RZ

Egyptian Art: Drawings and Paintings
first published in 1972 as *Egyptian Drawings*
by Octopus Books Limited

Text © copyright 1972 Artia, Prague
Illustrations © copyright 1972 Werner Forman

All rights reserved. No part of this publication
may be reproduced, stored in a retrieval system.,
or transmitted in any form or by any means,
electronic, mechanical, photocopying, recording
or otherwise, without the permission of the
copyright holder and the Publisher.

ISBN 0 600 55277 2
Printed in Czechoslovakia by Polygrafia, Prague
2/02/04/51-02

CONTENTS

The term "Egyptian drawing" needs more precise definition. Drawing from Ancient Egypt is not recognized as an independent art form. It is strictly preparatory and as such is classed with the finished work, but it is, in addition, a product of the observation of nature (see the animal drawings in this book). One can see how, through the drawing, a continual flow of fresh reality has invaded the invention and been artistically elaborated. Perhaps the same process can be perceived in the genre scenes of Eighteenth Dynasty tomb pictures and in the lost domestic paintings, a conclusion suggested by the so-called sketchbooks of the figurative artists of this period. Drawing was not an independent art form in the modern sense, and not to be thought of as graphic art, or separate from painting. Egyptian drawing was not meant to be reproduced. The frequent appearance of identical motifs, for example on paintings in different tombs or on vignettes in the Books of the Dead, is merely the result of conventions governing tomb decoration.

Egyptian drawing is related to painting in character, but the ground on which drawings and paintings were executed differ. Painting is mostly found on a stucco base or a loam plaster, whereas papyrus served as a ground for drawing. However, there is no clear dividing line between paintings and drawings, for, as the reader of this book will soon notice, the drawings on papyrus are also paintings, while the master-sketches in the tombs are drawings rather than paintings. The transition from drawing to painting is a fluid one. The line which is a characteristic of drawing takes on a form-creating energy in painting: it outlines the painted figure, confines it and forms a framework for it. A drawing, too, had to be coloured, and the approach to colour in the drawing was no different from that adopted in painting. There were no differences in degree between painting and drawing on the one hand and the sketch on the other, at least not for the Ancient Egyptian artist. A sketch can be a design for a painting and is often a work of such aesthetic perfection that it deserves our interest. The firmly drawn lines, mostly in black and red, come close to the modern concept of drawing.

The sketch-books of Ancient Egyptian artists give a clear indication of how laborious every beginning is. In this volume we turn to these sketch-books with interest, as they also contain miniatures of daily life and technical experiments.

Originally art was not free. In substance and ideologically it was subordinate to non-artistic purposes. But man's urge to create, which manifests itself in his art, can raise even a ritual object to the level of a work of art. This does not preclude such ritual objects from becoming a means of exerting influence, for instance in the hands of priests, but this has nothing to do with the work of art. Its function is a secondary concern, and does not lessen its value as an aesthetic object.

Ancient Egyptian works of art resulted from the needs of the religion. In the early days their main purpose was to illustrate a belief in man's reincarnation after death and this preoccupation influenced the choice of colour, form and material. Even the original site, tomb or temple, bears evidence of this approach.

The limitations of Egyptian art make it difficult to establish suitable evaluative criteria for judging it. The appreciation of European art stems from the teachings of the Greeks and there is still a school of thought which underrates the Ancient Egyptians. The art of the twentieth century has, however, introduced new styles of perception and treatment which help us to find a new approach to Ancient Egyptian art as well. There is no denying that the treatment and purpose of a piece of sculpture as famous as the Village Sheikh in the Egyptian Museum in Cairo is prescribed, first and foremost, by the religion: the function of a statue is to continue the dead man's existence in the Other World. But behind all this there is the genius of the anonymous wood-carver. He must have been aware of the aesthetic effect that his work would have and may perhaps have conveyed this to his client. The creation of outstanding works of art is inconceivable without the involvement of a powerful degree of aesthetic awareness. Herein lie the prerequisites for even a modern spectator to be moved by the aesthetic form and the charm of an ancient Egyptian work of art and admire the workmanship of an unknown artist. Every work of art as it were takes the spectator into partnership.

Ancient Egyptian art belongs to a highly developed culture that is alien to us and is subject to laws of its own. Two categories are found, each with its respective principle of form: sculpture in the round and the picture on one plane, in high or low relief, in painting or drawing. We will consider this last group as one unit, for Egyptian relief is subject to the same laws of form as painting or drawing. As these two art forms are functionally related, it seems relevant to say a few words here about the principles of form and their treatment.

The early stages of Egyptian art are linked with the founding and setting up of the Egyptian state. By about 2700 BC formulas for one-dimensional art and sculpture had been worked out and these rules remained valid throughout the prehistoric period in Egypt, which lasted some three thousand years. Vital political and ideological revolutions (such as that of Akhenaten in c. 1380 BC) did not affect the basic approach. The inherited forms were given a new content and the visual approach changed, so much so that it seems right to label the period of Akhenaten as a special phenomenon in Egyptian art history. Strong elements of sensuality widened its artistic range without changing the basic conventions (observe the rendering of face and fingers in Fig. 36). This adherence to form has earned the Ancient Egyptians the reputation of being incorrigibly conservative. Development within the history of Egyptian art can indeed be shown to have resulted not from the abandonment of the inflexible academic style, but from modifications to it.

In the Old Kingdom the most important patronage of artists and craftsmen occurred in the Memphis region, which was the ruling centre. It was in Memphis that the pyramid towns and the monumental necropolis with its vast demand for works of art were to be found. The local god of Memphis, Ptah, became the patron of all craftsmen and artists. He it was who, according to Memphetic theology, created men, deities and all creatures. His every deed was that of an artist. His significance can be judged by the politically and ideologically exposed position of his high priests. For in the New Kingdom this post was the second most important office in the priesthood throughout the land. His full title was "Supreme Master of all Craftsmen and Artists". The fact that the patron of artists was also the local god of the capital city suggests that artists and their work enjoyed a high status.

•

SCULPTURE

It seems inappropriate that a picture such as an Egyptian drawing should be included with "plastic art", even though graphic skills were of great importance in the sculpture process, in the individual phases of sketching and transferring to the stone. Sculpture, relief, and painting (and therefore also drawing on the

I Jar with red figures, Naqada II culture: baked clay, c. 3300 BC

Jar with red figures from the Naqada II culture
Cairo

These pottery jars with red figures are considered to be typical of the first all-Egyptian stage of culture in the prehistoric era (Naqada II, c. 3300 BC). The scenes are given against a light-coloured clay background. The range of subject-matter is wide. As here, depictions of animals are often found: four ostriches, a crocodile to the side, two scorpions at the top, on the shoulder of the vessel. Elsewhere there are pictorial accounts of historical events, which make these jars of particular interest to archaeologists. Another characteristic feature of this pottery is the wavy lines running from the shoulder to the bottom of the jar.

unfinished tomb wall) all served the same purpose of preserving elements of worldly reality for the afterlife, so for a thorough understanding of this approach to art let us include a brief outline of the nature and purpose of a sculpture.

The depiction of man in sculpture is based on the hypothesis that there is a syntactical relationship between the image and the prototype. Just as a divinity lives in his temple pictures through a ritual act, so a man can by means of a ritual instil a certain physical principle, a part of his soul (his *ka*) into a statue of himself. Thereby he hopes to extend the limits set for his life on earth, to encompass the eternity for which he longs.

This idea first found concrete expression in tombs. A small chamber, called *Serdab*, was set aside for the statue of the owner of the tomb. In his stone body, his "substitute" body, the dead man was present at the sacrifices to his *ka*. For this *ka* required nourishment. In the course of time ritual replaced actual sacrifice, and it was sufficient for the requisite objects to be shown in word or image inside the tomb. Ritual magically made them functional.

Let us look first at the laws underlying Egyptian sculpture. There were four ways in which a man could be depicted: standing, sitting, crawling or squatting. From these basic postures are derived virtually all the possible representations of human beings in Egyptian sculpture, whether they were divinities, kings, men, women, or children. The first impression of Egyptian sculpture is one of peace and dignity, as manifestations of permanence. Although the bodies are not conceived as organic entities, the restrained energy of a muscle on the upper arm or the suggestion of a smile on the lips gives to the whole an impression of grandeur and unusual liveliness. This is, undoubtedly, a reflection of the genius of the skilled artist. To modern eyes this attempt to adhere to the academic laws and yet give to the functional sculptured object the aura of a work of art deserves the highest praise. Examples here are the work of the Scribe of the Louvre or the Village Sheikh in the Cairo Egyptian Museum.

Every Egyptian sculpture is conceived and created for a particular setting. The effect of such a sculpture is enhanced by its surroundings, the place where it stands, the space around it, and the timelessness the sculptor has sought to capture in its creation. This feeling of a space of its own is created by the use of a plinth or base support, without which an Egyptian sculpture is unthinkable. In the case of stone statues part of the material remains in the form of a pillar and both the seemingly forward-stepping leg and the arms are only partly released from the stone. Work of this kind is not incomplete, but the "right" view was from the front.

This clarifies a further characteristic of Egyptian sculpture: it is intended to be seen from the front. Other aspects are a sense of grandeur achieved through its restfulness and an admirable paring down to essentials in characterization and type. By type, we mean the stylization of the face that corresponds to the standard model at any given time. This was always the face of the pharaoh himself. So it is quite possible to speak of portraits from the time of Ramesses II or the era of Tuthmosis III.

Egyptian artists did also, on the other hand, use great delicacy in individual characterization. The slim, youthful, ageless bodies formed part of the style, or rather the Ancient Egyptian ideal, of the human body.

The demand for a personal likeness ran counter to this. The *ba* part of the human soul has to be able to leave his *ka* statue, his substitute body, and find it again. Hence the vital role of the name. It is an indispensable prerequisite of any sculpture.

This discrepancy between the ideal and the true likeness led to the suppression of signs of age. Thus stylized folds on the chest will depict the flabby and withering skin of an older man. Here and there real portraiture can, however, be detected. The clothing reflects the trends of fashion at the time and for the archaeologist today acts as an important means of dating the sculptures.

The logical outcome of this demand for a life-like *ka* statue (a picture based on life) and ageless representation is two statues for any one person, each corresponding to a desired image. The person depicted obviously had to sit as model for the artist who made his *ka* statue. This is clear from tomb reliefs even from the Old Kingdom.

The portraits of pharaohs were not always made according to the prescribed formulae. The Middle Kingdom and the Amarna period opened up entirely new possibilities. Throughout the history of Egyptian art the ideal of timeless sculpture is preserved in its purest form in the statues of gods. To the modern visitor Egyptian sculpture seems closer to nature than one-dimensional works because it is more true to life.

THE PICTURE ON ONE PLANE

Relief and painting originated in tombs and temples side by side with sculpture. In the long corridors and chambers the painted reliefs or murals tell the visitor of life and daily existence in Ancient Egypt — work in the fields throughout the year; the activities of leather-workers, goldsmiths, builders, sculptors, painters and officials; the entertainments of the rich owners of the tombs, who are themselves shown sympathetically watching the various craftsmen working.

The scenes appear in rows, as if on a lined sheet, one after the other and one above the other, and all are turning towards the owner of the tomb. He is an enormous figure, compared to the others, in accordance with his social status. The horizontal sequence of events stretches along the entire height of the main figure. The scenes should be looked at, or rather read, in the same manner as they were conceived — as a narrative, a sequence of events.

The skill of the individual artists can be seen in the composition of each picture, the use of colour and the choice of subject-matter, as well as in the brushwork. The same themes keep appearing — the return of the flocks, a pleasure-trip into a papyrus-thicket, hunting scenes, revelry — without any discernible principle of selection. During the course of Egyptian history the number and variety of themes permissible for tomb decorations increased. These glimpses of Egyptian daily life, a treasure trove for the archaeologist, offered the Egyptians themselves, via their ritual, a guarantee of undisturbed future existence, with all their material needs provided. In other words, the scenes preserved life itself.

Apart from this religious concept there was also, in the New Kingdom, an aesthetic interest that encouraged visits to tombs and temples. This pragmatic approach was expressed in inscriptions in which the dead owner of the tomb turned to the spectator, asking him not to forget to offer a prayer for his well-being when looking at this "pure and beautiful" monument.

In spite of the fact that the one-plane picture conveys scenes from life, its style and form are alien to a concept of lifelikeness. Yet anyone who has learnt to look at Expressionism, and its successor movements such as Futurism, can find in Egyptian one-dimensional art the same feeling for and awareness of the laws of planes. The unusual way in which the human body is represented results from this awareness. It is, as it were, built up of a series of different views. The figures are invariably shown with their head in profile but their eye as if seen from the front; the shoulders are represented frontally, the chest in three-quarter view and the waist again from the front, but with a navel in three-quarter position; the buttocks, legs and arms are shown in profile and both arms and both legs have to be visible. This applies both to standing and to walking figures.

The rules of perspective did not apply and the third dimension was totally banned, at least from official art in the tombs and temples. Perspective was a principle not demanded in the realistic reproductions of life required for tombs and temples. Nevertheless, some artists did master its elements. The sketchbooks, which will be discussed later, contain many observations and experiments which do not belong at all to the sphere of official and commissioned art.

Certain modifying trends can be detected in the history of Egyptian art. They occurred in the period of the New Kingdom, and particularly at the time of the Pharaohs Amenophis II, Tuthmosis IV and Amenophis III and increased considerably during the period of his successor Akhenaten. Under Ramesses II similar trends seem to have existed. The search for modified stylistic elements and their explanation are particularly evident during the final period, in the tomb of Queen Nefertiti.

The principle of "sequence" adopted in present-day art has a predecessor in Egyptian one-dimensional painting, where a group of soldiers marching side by side or figures sitting side by side were popular subjects. The bodies offered a pleasing impression of harmony because they were depicted in a row, with each slightly overlapping the next, the separate figures being distinguished by colour shading.

The need to portray work in progress led to the depiction of twisted limbs or movement, which meant that the logical dynamics of work often came into conflict with the statically designed composite body. The figures seen in movement are mostly slaves. From the outset they were portrayed in a less strictly "academic" manner, since the cult of the dead did not involve any of them.

Various renowned Egyptologists have tried to express in words the peculiarities of this flat manner of depiction. Heinrich Schäfer and, later, Emma Brunner-Traut have unquestionably succeeded in capturing all its essential features in their respective terms "geradansichtig-vorstellig" and "aspektivisch", literally "straight-seeing" and "aspectivist". It was not until linear perspective in Classical Greek art broadened the flat plane in depth that a new era in art began, and the western world has, until recently, been guided by it. For the Ancient Egyptian artist of that time the sensual, physical charm of Greek art must have presented a major temptation, but official Egyptian art severely ignored everything Greek.

Some three hundred years ealier the rulers of the Twenty-sixth Dynasty had organized a renaissance of Classical Egyptian art with a concentration of all intellectual ability. After the unsettled history of the preceding period, when various foreign rulers held sway, resuscitation of the glorious past, whose stone

II Head of a king: drawing on limestone, c. 1120 BC

Painters' Sketchbooks and Pupils' Practice Books
Cairo

The method used on the limestone ostracon is similar to that used in the sphere of high art. First a sketch was made in red, then black was used for correction. In the case of pupils' practice books this last phase clearly reveals the helping hand of an experienced master. The number of heads of pharaohs surviving on limestone pictures is considerable, but whole-figure sketches are less frequent. In one such work by a pupil the king wears a blue crown, as at the time of Amenophis III. It is adorned with the Uraeus serpent, the royal diadem. A hieroglyphic inscription runs down over the broken edge: "Pharaoh of Upper Egypt... (Lower Egypt is missing), Ruler of the Two Lands". The broken edge in the lower third was used as a work surface. Ribbons are dangling from the pharaoh's neck. Probably the trainee painter wished to test the effect of a band of inscription running alongside the figure. The drawing itself bears marks of hasty work. The pupils would have been aware of the tricky nature of the highly absorbent material and tried to prevent the paint spreading by drawing quickly. No corrections can be seen. The work seems to have been rejected.

13

monuments were there for all to see, must have been useful, particularly for internal political reasons. Yet after the Saite Renaissance ageing Egypt surrendered to the young Greek spirit in the typical Egyptian manner; it assimilated new concepts. This synthesis gave the last and decisive impulse to the final acceptance of realism in Egyptian art. But the function of realistic sculpture remained identical to that of Ancient Egypt; it was intended to be a substitute stone body for the person depicted.

Let us turn first to the renaissance in the Twenty-fifth and Twenty-sixth Dynasties, when there were great achievements in the fine arts. Works came into being that were similar in form and concept to those of the classical era. Yet between the Saite Period and the era that served as its model there was a gap of more than one thousand years of political and social development. A firm Egyptian rule had to be established to protect the style, in view of the unsettled political conditions. The old attitude towards sculpture and one-dimensional pictures had to be recaptured. A similar situation existed at the beginning of the Middle Kingdom when, following upon decisive political events, the craftsmanship and taste of the Old Kingdom had been lost. At that time the artists in the necropolis near Memphis were forced to study the masters of the Old Kingdom and to copy their work. In the case of the early Middle Kingdom, this method proved successful, as it was a question of recapturing a lost form in a land that had firmly fenced itself off from the surrounding world.

By the Twenty-sixth Dynasty the situation had changed. Egypt had opened up towards the world and with the advent of foreign conquerors foreign taste had poured into the land. It required a good deal of help, in spite of the far-reaching study of earlier masters, to make, say, a typically Egyptian statue. The result is smooth, faultless works. They are technically more perfect than their classical models but most of them lack the tension that creates a work of art. The application of new techniques to earlier models affected the end product. This combination seems to have become more complicated as the influence of Greek culture on Egypt increased and offered an alternative Greek art.

WORKING METHOD

What we call "models" must have been specially made for the sculptors of the fourth century. Feet, arms and heads of pharaohs, fashioned according to stringent laws of proportion, could be used by the sculptor to measure exact proportions. They were even marked in figures on the pieces. These models are incomplete as they were intended only as guides for the remaining chiselled work. To judge by the places where they have been found, these measuring aids were used exclusively by the schools of sculpture in Lower Egypt.

Similar patterns for sculptors date from the Saite Renaissance. For example, figures of gods in typical postures and garments were intended to convey the impression of monumentality and axiality in classical sculpture. Reliefs included hieroglyphs made to faultless perfection. One gathers that the artist was being guided towards the Egyptian "viewpoint". One extremely interesting field is opened up by the system of lines that was at that time designed for Egyptian sculptors. This had a long tradition, for even in the Old Kingdom the artist's work was simplified by a system of lines, though it differed fundamentally from the elaborate network of squares used during the Saite Renaissance.

A few words should be said here about the way in which the Egyptian sculptor worked. The human body and the interrelated proportions of its individual component parts were laid down according to a canon of proportions that was mathematically balanced. These rules for the construction of a figure were laid out within a geometrical grid on the drawing paper, over an imaginary base line, or, alternatively, all four planes would be drawn with lines and markings. After this rough sketch the sculptor penetrated into the stone evenly from all four sides till he uncovered the figure. In this way the sculpture, though incomplete in treatment, is complete at every stage, at least within itself. And there are examples of such statues being quickly painted and put to use in spite of their being incomplete. Perhaps the client had died unexpectedly, or perhaps the financial situation had worsened.

This certainty of approach on the part of the Old Kingdom artists is often attributed to the fact that the possibilities for creating form were not disturbed by any internal or external influences.

The art of the Middle Kingdom, as previously stated, emphasized the forms of the Old Kingdom and no changes in working methods can be detected. During excavations by the German Orient Society at Amarna, the city of the reformer Akhenaten, a complete sculptor's workshop was discovered. The most sensational find was, beyond any doubt, the famous bust of Queen Nefertiti. On the ruined shelves lay various unfinished statues, from which one can deduce the methods used by sculptors working a thousand years after the Mycerinus statues were carved. The number of lines had increased, if anything, and we gain the impression of a struggle for the proper form, for the correct proportions. For the reforms initiated by the pharaoh Akhenaten left their imprint on the work of artists as well. A new style was being created and this demanded substantially more lifelikeness than had been required of the sculptors of the preceding periods. Apart from the new political situation, there was a new social climate, and the experiences the Egyptians had acquired during a thousand years of citizenship left their mark. Mycerinus sculptors do not seem to have been "sickened with pallid doubt". The torso of an Amarna princess (Berlin: Inv. No 21 254) is covered with a profusion of black lines. Even the subsidiary lines have increased in number, for they were important in helping the sculptor to achieve the correct measurements. The increased number of lines doubtless made his work easier, but their meaning may have been kept secret and handed down from father to son. This is suggested by the testimony of a Middle Kingdom sculptor called Irtj-sen who boasts on his stela of secret knowledge.

In the Saite Period this increased use of proportionally correct working aids indicates a frenetic urge to attain the prescribed norm, and indeed we get the impression that the right proportions were considered more important than the resulting sculpture. The network system came into regular use as an aid. The figure was inscribed within a system of squares that interlink like the meshes of a net. This type of treatment is not an invention of the Saite Period, for it was an old tradition in Egypt and resulted from the working methods discussed in connection with the Mycerinus figures. The body of the figure was executed according to a fixed canon of proportion, based on the fist, which represented one small ell (a quarter of the standard ell). The height of the figure was calculated as being eighteen small ells and the width across the shoulders was four small ells. An alternative system of measurement, again taken from the human body, was based on a hand's breadth (across the tips of the fingers). The height of a standing figure would be shown to be twenty-seven hands' breadth and his shoulders six hands' breadth across. The sculptor marked out his stone into squares, using the figure's fist as his basic unit, or one side of the square. Thus a standing figure was always drawn within a grid eighteen squares high by four squares wide.

The scale of the figures changed as the grid was made larger or smaller but the proportions were not affected. This meant that even artists of little talent could sculpt or paint successfully. Little was left to chance; the outline of the figure would be projected from the sketchbook, where it was inscribed in this network of squares, onto a wall that was again covered by squares. This technique perhaps explains why nearly all the tombs show evidence of sound craftsmanship, for the artistic level did not drop from a given standard even in times of political or social crisis. Some of the plates give details of this type of sculptural work on walls, showing both master-sketches and their final execution. They show the procedure involved, and thus complement the technical data given in this part of the book.

Various museums possess papyri with figures depicted in their ideal proportions, in elevation and groundplan. The papyrus collection in the Staatliche Museen in Berlin, for instance, possesses two of these precious items (Inv. No P 11 775, P 13 558). One of these includes a guide to executing a sphinx, which is presented both in groundplan and in elevation. The guide lines and various parts of the drawings are accompanied by marginal notes, perhaps explanations, or possibly figures. The same applies to a model of a leg in the Cairo Museum (Cat. Gen. 33337). It appears that no significant technical novelties were introduced during the Saite Period in sculpture, relief work or painting. The method by which a statue of the Late Period was executed did not differ from the process we have outlined for the Mycerinus sculptures of the Old Kingdom.

At all periods a relief or painting was executed in the following manner: first the walls were smoothed down by stone-masons; then, if a painting was to be executed, the next step involved the application of a layer of stucco covering the entire wall; then the contour draughtsman divided up the wall and inscriptions, illustrations of events or decorative strips were allotted their fixed places; finally the rough lines of the figures and the figures themselves were indicated within the network of squares. All of this had to correspond to the pattern (presumably on papyrus) that the artist had originally submitted to his client for approval.

Red seems to have been the colour generally used for the master-sketch. An example from the Old Kingdom (Mastaba of Kai-em-anch) confirms this rule by offering an exception: here the master used yellow and his sketch served as a preliminary to the master-sketch, which was done in red.

Where master-sketches have survived they reveal great talent. They are aesthetically highly effective and appeal directly to us today because we are accustomed to graphics and used to appreciating works without colour. Several examples of this can be seen in this book (e.g. Plates 10 and 11). Black paint was used for corrections; in other words, it was applied at a later stage. Beneath the network of lines we can often see evidence of the artist's painstaking search for the correct form (cf. Plates 16—20).

III Scene of daily life — man and goats: drawing on limestone, c. 1120 BC

Painters' Sketchbooks and Pupils' Practice Books
Cairo: Inv. No. J 69 408

This scene gives the impression of being a picture of daily life. A goat is feeding on the leaves of a tree while suckling its kid. A man comes along and seems angry about the damage the animal has caused. In his left hand he is holding an object and making a threatening gesture with it. The ostracon seems undamaged, for the artist has drawn part of his sketch on the less smooth sections of the stone. A base line indicates the lower edge of the picture. Although it is sketchy, this drawing does not give the impression of being a pupil's practice exercise. In all probability pupils rarely treated themes of their own free choice, but rather tended to practise subject-matter that formed standard tomb decorations. Here we seem to have an example of the lost painted decorations in private houses, where preference was given to scenes from everyday life.

The next stage of work on a relief would be carried out by the sculptor. He first outlined the red contour lines with a copper chisel and then began to chip away the surface round the figures. Slowly the scene would begin to stand out from the surface of the wall. This was the method adopted for high relief work, the most common type of relief in Egypt. For low relief the process was reversed; the outline of the figure stood out while the figure itself was sunk into the stone. In both types of relief the last phase of the sculptor's work involved modelling the actual figure. The sculptor, or possibly another craftsman, would burnish the grey stone, using sand and polishing stones. Finally the entire wall would be covered with a thin layer of white plaster. At that point the painter took over. He first outlined the contours of the relief in red; then another painter would paint the entire relief surface, beginning in most cases with the blue-grey background. Figures and details followed in the relevant colours. Thus painting added the final touch to relief work and sculpture.

The painter, working on the surface of the relief-covered wall, intensified the impression of plasticity that the sculptor had already created in modelling the relief. But no light and shade effects were applied on relief, or indeed on sculpture in general. The bas-reliefs on the external walls of the mighty temples are exceptions, since their design did include light and shade to create a visual effect. The colourfulness of tombs and temples once presented a feast for the eyes, but today both reliefs and sculptures are merely stone-coloured.

The only place where this indispensable collaboration between sculptor and painter did not occur is on the rock-tombs at Thebes, where the brittleness of the rock made it impossible to work in relief. The tombs therefore had to be decorated exclusively with paintings. Thanks to this external factor paintings of great beauty came into existence and painting became the major form of art in the New Kingdom. Its development can be clearly traced in the tombs of officials at the courts of Amenophis II and Amenophis III. The difference in style between the tombs dating from the time of Tuthmosis III and those of his next-but-one successor is very striking.

The technique of applying paint was similar to that adopted on relief work, except that the layer of stucco was applied onto the smooth surface of the stone. This was then coated with plaster made of Nile mud. Otherwise the method of working was identical, apart from the omission of the relief. First the master-sketch was drawn out and then it was executed in colour.

THE ROLE OF COLOUR

Painting lives by colour. In Ancient Egypt the role of colour in art was probably originally determined once again by religion, for colour and painting as such were not intended to enhance the sensuous apperance of the person depicted. They were rather designed to have a symbolic value, and this continued to be understood even at a much later date. But awareness of the symbolic values of colour clearly did not lessen aesthetic appreciation, for delight in colour for its own sake is evident in articles dating from the New Kingdom. The rules of colour symbolism were probably part of the store of secret knowledge which was guarded by the learned priesthood and systematically passed on to the young apprentices in the art schools. When, in the Amarna period, the daring step was taken — interesting from the point of view of art history — from flat, conventional polychromy to a more expressive use of colour, it was the priesthood, still loyal to the old gods and opposed to Akhenaten's religious reforms and the art that reflected his ideas, which preserved the knowledge of colour symbolism until the Nineteenth Dynasty, when the old cults were restored. The colouring of pictures dating from this later period, therefore, reveals a close affinity to the conventional usage of the pre-Amarna period.

The basic colours of Egyptian art were black, white, red, yellow, green and blue. In their symbolic values they represented the following objects and concepts:

Black stood for the fruitful earth, night, death and the underworld. It was also frequently used for the skin colour of the inhabitants of the Other World.

White belonged to anything festive, such as the garments of high-ranking people, while servants and foreigners wore coloured clothes. White was also used to convey solemnity, as demonstrated by the crown of Upper Egypt, which was made from white leather. Certain sacred animals, such as baboons, a kind of bull and a cow, owed their special role in the cult to the white colouring of their bodies. White was also used to indicate persons of pure character.

Red denoted anything unrestrained or dangerous, or extremes of rage. It also represented disorder and evil. Such notions were associated, for example, with foreigners, the desert and Seth, the god of foreigners and the desert, all of which were represented in red. Even the name of the god was written in red. In the "dream-books" bad days were marked in red and good days in black. Plutarch reported that this superstitious fear of red reached such extremes that red-haired foreigners were burnt in El Kab. Sources from the pre-Greek period also suggest that redheads were registered.

Green meant freshness and prosperity. The resurrected god Osiris was therefore often painted in green. The amulets which were said to protect the body and make it invulnerable were produced from green faience or painted green in illustrations.

Blue symbolized the celestial, the heavenly. It was used as the colour of the skin of the universal gods Amon, Amon-Ra and Re-Harachte, as well as of the beards and wigs of their own divine families and related families.

Yellow, the colour of gold, also signified immortality. It was, naturally, employed in the painting of jewels, symbols of power such as crowns and diadems, and the sun and moon.

The dictionary of the Egyptian language interprets the word "colour" as meaning "external apperance of a god, kind, being, character". This group of hieroglyphs is depicted either by an animal pelt or by hair. This is a pointer to the sphere of sensuous perception and seems to be the linguistic and logical way of distinguishing objects, and in particular human beings, from one another. In this respect its time of origin is a fitting one, for the era of the pyramid builders, the Old Kingdom, when works of art were produced collectively, knew nothing of this. It was the First Intermediate Period that followed the Old Kingdom and its disintegration that created individualism in Egypt. A large number of new words which are to be found in texts from this period confirm this. Among them is the concept of colour, which encompasses the meaning both of external nature and of character.

The following rules of colouring became valid for the human figure: men were depicted with a reddish-brown skin, women with yellow-ochre skin. Hair was generally painted black, while garments were white with coloured accessories which corresponded to the use of various materials such as gems, semi-precious stones, faience, shells and precious metals. Fauna and flora were reduced to basic colours. Paint was applied unblended and was sometimes thinned down. It did not reproduce the colours of the original in nature but rather the *idea* of the natural image according to the established conventions of art. The effect of light and shade was not taken into consideration. Nevertheless, the use of different colours for the same object can be seen within the same text: for example, the same object may be reproduced in the hieroglyphic script in different colours. The colours change from red to yellow, blue to green or blue to black. The reasons are either aesthetic or stem from the symbolic values of the objects depicted in the hieroglyphs. In the Old and Middle Kingdoms harsh colours were placed side by side. Only in the New Kingdom, and especially during the reign of Amenophis III, can we detect an attempt to make a transition from one colour to the next by letting one colour run into the neighbouring colour. But no new colours were invented. Mixed colours, which produce atmosphere, can only be found in paintings from El-Amarna. From the latter half of the Eighteenth Dynasty the shades of grey and brown appeared. But their symbolic significance for the Ancient Egyptians has not been discovered from the texts that have come down to us. Traces of the following colours can be discerned on a painter's palette of the New Kingdom in the Kestner Museum in Hanover (1951/54): light grey-blue, black, brick-red, ochre-yellow, grey blue, light blue and dark red.

Chemical tests have largely explained the composition of Egyptian paint. The English chemist A. Lukas did some thorough research in this field. The paint colours used by early Egyptian artists were natural colours. They consisted of pigments in natural minerals which were pulverized for this purpose. Black was produced from coal soot or charcoal, white from limestone (calcium carbonate) or gypsum (calcium sulphate). Red, brown and yellow were made from ferric oxide, ochre or mixtures of the two. Azurite provided the basic material for blue, malachite for green. In the New Kingdom, chemical colours for green and blue were developed as by-products when making coloured glass from a mixture of copper oxide, chalk or limestone, pulverized natron and silica in the form of quartz. The melted-down material was similarly finely pulverized and used as an effective colour pigment. Thus grey was produced from black and white, orange from red and yellow, and a pink shade from red and white. In the New Kingdom the colour scale was enriched by the use of gold pigment. The mixing of the basic colours appears to have differed from one period to another. Their composition was probably a workshop secret which was passed on from one generation to the next. The following materials can be detected as binding agents, generally thinned with water: resin, glue, gelatine, white of egg, gum arabic and, from the New Kingdom, beeswax. The binding agents made the colours insoluble in water after they had dried. Brushes were made by the painter himself from chewed plant fibres or the frayed midribs of palm-fronds.

Another technical problem should be mentioned at this point. Visitors to an Egyptian necropolis often ask how those underground labyrinths of corridors and chambers were lit. One thing is certain: the workers in the tombs must have had

IV The Last Judgment before Osiris: papyrus, between 1075 and 950 BC

The Book of the Dead of the Lady Taucherit
Twenty-first Dynasty (from Thebes)
Nederlandsches Museum van Oudheden te Leyden: Cat. Leemans T.3

Published by C. Leemans, *Aegyptische hiëroglyphische lijkpapyrus, T. 3 van het Nederlandsche Museum van Oudheden te Leyden*, Leyden, 1882

This scene is taken from chapter 125 of the Book of the Dead of the Lady Taucherit. By this time the reorganization of the Last Judgment had already been accomplished. Each individual deity is named. On the right appears the god Thoth with writing utensils in his hand, in the middle Horus. Also to be seen is the name of the Lady Taucherit, who, wearing the fashionable dress of her time, is approaching from the left and is personally present at the act of weighing. The change in style that Egyptian art had undergone since the time of Amenophis III is clearly visible. The figures have become more real and more fragile. The media used, black paint and careful brushwork, are proof of this new trend.

sufficient light at their disposal, since the reliefs and paintings were not done in workshops but on the spot. Expert opinion dismisses the view that torches were used, since no trace of smoke has ever been found. What seems most likely is that mirrors were used to deflect daylight into the chambers. Tombs can still be lit in this fashion today.

THE PERSONALITY OF THE ARTIST: SKETCHBOOKS AND PRACTICE WORK

So far we have been discussing only the work of fully-trained artists. We cannot trace the development of any artist from the beginning of his apprenticeship to his full maturity for, as indicated in the catalogue, no Ancient Egyptian work of art bears a signature. The names of sculptors and painters are known only in the rarest cases, for conditions were similar to those in the Middle Ages. More detailed studies and analyses of style will have to be carried out if we are to attribute various masterpieces to the hand of the same artist.

The Egyptian artist enjoyed high esteem, far higher than that conferred on the artists of Ancient Greece and Rome. His status in society derives from the religious origin and purpose of his works. As research has shown, there was a close relationship in the Old Kingdom between the person who commissioned the work and his artist, and so the client would often make his own proposals for the design of his tomb. The children of men in high places would adopt titles from the sphere of the fine arts and they showed great pride in the use of these titles, which ranked not far behind those used at court. Even men engaged in politics, such as the viziers Mereruka and Chentika, allowed themselves to be portrayed as painters of the seasonal deities at their tomb entrances. To what extent this was prompted by some religious motive, or whether it was simply a product of purely artistic creativity cannot be determined. There is an obvious relationship with the new forms of sanctuaries being built at the time for the sun-god Ra, in which portraits of the seasonal gods in the so-called season chambers also form a relief cycle with scenes of events in the season-bound lives of men and animals.

It was always the Treasury of a king or a temple, such as the temples of Ptah in Memphis or of Amon in Thebes, which commissioned large projects from artists or craftsmen. Viziers and other high officials were granted tombs with enormous relief-decorated rooms arranged in a row as if a sort of royal honour. In fact, the cost of a tomb and its furnishings creamed off a large proportion of the wealth created by the community. In the Old and Middle Kingdoms, at least, it was the king who transferred large commissions for the construction of tombs to the royal Treasury. The whole operation was set in motion, administered and supervised from here. The exploitation of quarries and ore mines was a royal privilege. The rock and mineral resources extracted from them, therefore, were not freely available to anyone.

The treasurer was put in charge of the craftsmen and artists engaged in a project, as is evident from a painting in Paser's tomb at Thebes-West. In it, craftsmen and artists are engaged in wood and metal work. In a marginal note to the scene, the treasurer calls to them: "Greetings to you, craftsmen! Be silent, for the vizier enters!" In another place the treasurer Dehutj says of himself: "I managed the craftsmen and artists..." It follows from the context that he was responsible for the working of gold, silver, electron, precious stones and other materials into artistic objects and utensils.

Less frequently the vizier, the royal chief master-builder and a high priest of the god Ptah, the patron of artists and craftsmen, had, according to evidence in texts, a direct control over the profession of craftsmen and artists. In exceptional cases, as, for example, in the Amarna period, artists also received direct instructions from the king himself. As a rule, the king was the instigator — as already mentioned — of artistic production. Responsibility for carrying it out was then delegated through the social hierarchy, from the officials of the highest rank, such as viziers, high priests of the god Ptah, the chief master-builder and the treasurer, who distributed the materials, down to the artists and craftsmen who actually did the work. The responsibility of the "managerial rank" for the artists was underlined by Ptahschepses, the high priest of Ptah, who was deeply concerned for them because of the special role of the god Ptah. He stressed: "... he was one of those ... who brought artists and craftsmen into favour with the king." The painter and the sculptor thus enjoyed considerable social status, though this may have applied only to outstanding masters. But one example is known of an artist being invited to a big hunting party. While the guests devoted themselves to the joys of the hunt, the painter lay in a papyrus boat and had himself entertained with beer and all manner of good things. This little scene is perhaps a substitute for a signature, for the artist immortalized himself in the tomb which had been built for the vizier Ptahhotep (Sixth Dynasty) in this way. There is an interesting statement concerning the relationship between client and artist in the same tomb. Here Ptahhotep says: "I encouraged the artists who made this tomb to praise the god because I satisfied them in everything they required from me in order to be glorified by the god." The artist was thus given a key role in ensuring the continued existence of the dead in the Other World. He created important prerequisites for a dead person's state of "glorification" by preparing a statue as a substitute "body for eternity" and a tomb, with its important ritual decor and furnishings, as a "house for eternity". The vizier seems to have provided for the artists himself on account of his high position, although the commission had been given by the king.

The idea that art has its origins in craftsmanship still remains deeply rooted in our minds. Artistic creativity, therefore, was probably regarded by the Ancient Egyptians merely as a special aspect of the craftsman's skill. Evidence for this is provided by a number of indicators. First of all, there was no special word for "art" or "artist", "craft" or "craftsman" in the Egyptian vocabulary. The same terms were used for the wood-, stone- and metal-processing trades.

The starting point in becoming an artist or craftsman consisted in acquiring the technical skills to be able to handle the appropriate materials and — as it seems to us today — the imperfect tools available as well. Both craftsmen and artists created objects whose perceived value depended on whether they were to be used merely in daily life or as important accessories in cult ceremonies. In this way, craftsmen such as joiners, leather-workers, producers of vases and goldsmiths could work alongside sculptors in large workshops. When faced with such a traditional scene depicting the work of craftsmen and artists as that in the tomb of Ni-anch-Pepi (Sixth Dynasty), the observer is hard put to it to distinguish between the different skills when exhorted to "Look at the work of sculptors and painters" and "Look at the work of craftsmen". These are, in fact, one and the same. The distinction between craftsmen and artists was probably not important.

Within the different vocations followed by Egyptian artists, there were certain specializations which were determined by the materials used and the kinds of objects created. Among these were workers in gold (or goldsmiths), sculptors and statue sculptors (the actual term was "bone-cutters"). This compound designation referred to sculptors in soft material, while the term "stone-borer" probably indicated a sculptor in hard material. The phrases "life restorer" and "he who maketh alive" for sculptors arose out of the role played by sculpture in mankind's continued existence in the Other World in accordance with the current religious beliefs. A specialist who produced figurative illustrations and hieroglyphs in stone according to the layout provided in a preliminary sketch was called a "relief-sculptor". A "copy-scribe" probably transferred the text drafts from the ostracon to the papyrus or on to the wall. A "draughtsman" followed sketched designs to outline the sequence of scenes and texts on the wall for the relief-sculptors. The craftsmen in this vocational group also probably participated in expensive expeditions to quarries in order to mark the blocks to be cut out of the rock. In the administrative records on the artists, their workplace is also mentioned in addition to their names and titles and their profession, for example, "NN, draughtsman from the settlement of craftsmen/artists at the Amon Temple [in Thebes] who is engaged in the Sokar Temple at this time".

At some point individual schools must have existed in Egypt. It is hard to prove this today, but in all probability they existed in the main towns, in provincial princely residences and in the great cultural centres.

The career of a painter's apprentice, who could also qualify as a sculptor, began in the workshop of the big building projects. In the necropolis of the officials and kings of the New Kingdom at Thebes-West, for instance, he first had to learn how to handle a brush and paint. The Egyptian scribe and the painter usually had two colours on their palette and it is these colours that predominate in the "practice books" used by painter's apprentices. How difficult it must have been to acquire this basic knowledge is shown on some ostraca found on rubbish heaps near the tombs of the pharaohs, especially those of Ramesses VI and Ramesses IX, and in the workmen's settlements in the Theban necropolis. Mastery of a rapid and firm brush-stroke was the first step towards grasping basic methods of composition and ways of putting them into practice. For these ostraca were made of highly absorbent limestone. The great contrast between the burning hot temperatures during the day and the cool nights in winter caused the limestone of the mountain ranges along the Nile to crumble in thin layers. Its surface is extremely smooth and very white. It was this material that gave beginners their practice books. On many of them we can see the first lines which, as in relief, are incised along an outline drawing in red.

Work on ostraca, which are known as "practice books", proceeded as follows: the master stated the subject-matter and drew a sketch; then the apprentices had to copy the sketch, first outlining it in red, striving anxiously to obtain the correct form. Mastery of the Egyptian canon of proportions must have caused great difficulties, for even the work of experienced pupils often gives an impression of

V The Last Judgment and Hall of Osiris: papyrus, between 305 and 30 BC

The Book of the Dead of Djoser, Priest of the Goddess of Love Bastet
Ptolemaic Period
Cairo (from Saqquara)

Illustrations V and 60 belong to a series of pictures from chapter 125 of the Book of the Dead. The content of this chapter is described in detail in the captions to Plates 39—42. The layout of the scene, however, has been changed, in particular with regard to the people involved. Osiris' assessors, the forty-two Judges of the Dead, are present and visible. The course of events is no longer split up into individual scenes, as was the case in the same scene in Kenna's Book of the Dead. The dead man is entering from the right, led by a goddess. He raises his arms towards Osiris in a gesture of worship, and then waits in humble obeisance for the result of the weighing on the great Balance. Horus (with a falcon head) and Anubis (with a jackal head) act as attendants at the Balance. Their names and titles, together with those of the dead man, can be read on a band of inscription. Thoth, the ibis-headed god of wisdom, who carries writing utensils, is noting down minutes of the proceedings. On his palette two colours can be clearly distinguished. His name and title are also given. They are to be found above his head, visually well-placed on a band of writing. In front of Thoth sits the soul-eating beast. The action continues in Plate 60.

clumsiness (Plate 2). Either the pupil corrected his own work in black or else this was done by an experienced painter. White was apparently used for correcting only when teachers dealt with the work of pupils who had completed their training.

There seem to be few examples of a picture being first confined within a frame and then subdivided (British Museum: 49 670). Some works by pupils are executed exclusively in black, though it is possible that correction lines cover the original drawing. All the themes for this type of work were taken from high art, heads of pharaohs being particularly frequent. But there is also practice work aimed at loosening the apprentice's wrist (for example, Berlin: 23 972 verso). Other examples show that script writing was practised.

Once the painter's apprentice had passed the first hurdle in mastering the simple techniques of his craft he had to begin to understand the idea behind the picture, which traditionally served as decoration for a tomb or a temple. He probably had pattern-books which he could study so as to broaden his knowledge, but unfortunately none of these pattern-books has survived. References to them can be found in the inscription of Irtj-sen (now in the Louvre: C 14). In this inscription are listed the motifs of pictures whose layout and execution must be mastered by an artist. Movement motifs, mentioned in three different variants, seem to be of some importance. First, a man walking, with one leg making a great stride forward; second, a woman walking, with a smaller step forward. The more restrained movement here is undoubtedly due to the discomfort caused by a fashion which required noble women to wear a very tight dress with shoulder straps. Working women, such as the wives of peasants, were shown making the natural, unrestricted movements that were appropriate to their various activities. The third movement motif is the "double-quick step", a vigorous movement made, for instance, by the king when killing his enemies. The bibliography at the temple of Edfu also contains such a work. One of the side chambers of the big forecourt of the Edfu temple contained a library and it has an inscription over the door stating this. Lists of books are inscribed on the walls, including the following: "Book about Red", "Book on Old Scripts for Work", "Instruction on Painting the Wall and Paying Heed to Bodily Form".

In tracing the few sources that indicate the existence of pattern-books, we find references as early as the Fifth Dynasty. If the interpretation of the relief in his tomb is correct, the vizier Mereruka is seen working on a design for the royal Sun Temples. On one stele King Neferhotep (Thirteenth Dynasty) recounts that he caused the figure of the god Osiris to be depicted exactly as he had found it on an old papyrus in his library.

A similar reference can be found in the Temple of Ramesses II at Abydos. It relates that the original designs for the statues of gods were drawn in the big inventory book by Thoth, the god of wisdom. Despite the mythical exaggeration of this statement, there is nevertheless an unambiguous reference here to pattern-books. It is possible to draw some conclusions from these few findings. Temples, palaces and building projects with large workshops and appropriate artists' studios possessed archives of specially devised pictorial and text patterns for use in the creation of religious literature and the decoration of tombs and temples. Among these patterns there were most likely collections of motifs, such as the movement motifs outlined by Irtj-sen, which had to be technically mastered by an artist.

Once the pupil had reached the status of assistant, he was set the task of collaborating on a major work. For he had to learn how to apply skilfully what he had mastered during his apprenticeship by studying and copying. The subject-matter was fixed, but there was a certain amount of latitude in how these themes were employed. The assistant also had to teach younger pupils. The high-point in his career came when he was appointed a foreman of sculptors, foreman of draughtsmen or foreman of painters. Such an appointment carried with it high social rank, as the examples of the sculptors Ipuki and Nebamun show, for they prepared magnificent tombs for themselves. Whole dynasties of artists existed. Records show that the office of "Foreman of the Painters of Amon" remained in one family for seven generations. The New Kingdom artists generally came under the Treasury. It was this institution, as in the case of the Amon Temple at Karnak, that commissioned artists.

Artists and their work are not mentioned very often, but with the growing individualization in Egyptian society evidence of the artist's conscious attitude to his work increased. Typically, more attention is paid to technical data than to skill in executing works of art. The latter must have been self-evident and therefore did not need to be mentioned. Thot, a leading sculptor of the Twenty-eighth Dynasty, boasts of having built houses. Ineni, an architect of the same dynasty, speaks of loam plaster as a background for paintings (his invention?) and mentions buildings in the temple of Karnak.

Somewhat different is the evidence of a painter in the later Ramesses period. He says of himself that he is a painter to whom no superior ever dared give instructions. On the contrary, he is a "draughtsman with skilful fingers from the Chnum-temple in Es, whom the High Priest in person had ordered to come to El-Kab". In conclusion it should be said that the artist's relationship with craftsmen often took the form of craftsmen and sculptors working side by side in the big workshops, where there would be carpenters, goldsmiths, leather-workers and many others.

The ostraca from the rubbish heaps and the settlements of the workers (now known as Deir el-Medina) did not only preserve pupils' practice books. Designs for murals and copies of existing works have been found, as well as occasional pictures in which the painter depicted specific situations. In content ostraca can be divided into:

1 Themes from high art, among them heads of kings and pictures with a religious meaning.

2 Copies. For example the drawing of the ugly Queen of Punt from the temple at Deir el-Bahri (Berlin: Inv. No. 21 442). The painter must have paid a visit there. The plump body of this queen did not tally with the Egyptians' ideal of beauty, which may have encouraged him to draw the picture.

3 Designs to be executed at a later stage on a wall. In the tomb of Senenmut we can see a portrait of a man which is clearly derived from an ostracon (Louvre: AF 184). Other such designs and their ultimate realization are known.

4 Subjects from lost house paintings. It is to be assumed that the Egyptians also adorned their houses with colourful decorations. But these houses were built of bricks made from Nile mud, which deteriorate with time and disintegrate rapidly. In this sphere completely different ideas were given pictorial form.

A favourite theme was that of the young mother. The women, with appropriate hairstyles, can be seen sitting on beds with a child by their side. Sometimes they are surrounded by sick-nurses. Other popular motifs, at least on ostracon patterns, include scenes with men and bulls or horses. It can therefore be assumed that such themes were also used in painting private houses (cf. Plate III).

5 Much space is taken up by pictures of occasional subjects. Here the rules of representation were frequently ignored. Particularly characteristic in this respect is the colour picture of a fruit-eating baboon (Berlin: Inv. No. 22 881). Picturesque scenes show dancing girls (Turin: 01 7052) or a horse resting (private collection). These last examples have considerable charm.

6 Animal fables and fairy-tales. Such pictures may have played an important role in Egypt, where people took delight in stories and knew many fairy-tales and fables. The little pictures related these stories in what today we would call comic strip form. On one of them a boy appears before a Mouse Judge and begs for pardon, his arms raised. Such a picture may have had a didactic aim. There are also illustrations to literature that have survived, for example illustrations to the Legend of Tefnut (Berlin: Inv. No. 21 443). Our catalogue includes one example (Plate 5).

7 Satire. Pictures of this type give the impression of glimpses into an inverted world. A mouse is sitting by a jug of wine; his hair is carefully styled and he is wrapped in elegant garments (Munich: 1549). This scene is modelled on one of the many toilet scenes in art and the irony is clear for all to see. One man is depicted at his toilet like a woman (who would appear normally in such scenes) and is also sucking wine through a straw. Such pictures may have been aimed at ridiculing the affluence of the age and the accompanying decline in morals. Obviously wars cannot be won with effeminate men of this type. And indeed even the victory-proud Egyptians suffered defeat after periods of great military successes. This would have been a difficult fact to explain to Ramesses II's Ministry of Propaganda, for, in a decisive battle against the Hittites the pharaoh achieved no more than a draw. Nevertheless, all pictures of this battle, as with those of the following period, continued to appear in the current manner with the pharaoh as victor. In fact the people may have thought of him differently. Another scene exists in which mice are overrunning a cat fort. This might well be an early attempt at political caricature. Scenes of this type are to be found on satirical papyri in Turin as well as on an ostracon in Berlin (2L 475 verso and recto).

8 Ostraca with caricatures of faces and with erotic pictures have also been found.

9 The last group includes works which painters made for themselves as a substitute for the expensive stelae (cf. Plate 9). On such pictures the artist is seen offering prayers to his god (for example, Leipzig: 1967 verso). The use of an ostracon as a stele substitute was adopted even by rich people. It is known that a man named Irinefer ordered an ostracon and underlined its function with his title and genealogy as a substitute for a tomb, in case the latter was destroyed. Here the ostracon assumed the function of a tomb and became a ritual object in the cult of the dead.

A word should be said here on the term "ostracon". It comes from the Greek and simply means a potsherd. The Egyptian word also included limestone fragments. It can be assumed that such ostraca were widely used all over Egypt.

BOOK PAINTING AND ILLUSTRATIONS

In Ancient Egypt books took the form of papyrus rolls. Illustrations to the various Books of the Dead, the best-known "book" of the early Egyptians, which are shown in this volume, cannot be considered as book paintings in the meaning of the term as applied to book paintings of the Middle Ages. The illustrations in the Books of the Dead are additions to the text. They are representations of what has already been given in the text and also illustrated in the tomb. Simply by being present, however, they contribute to the magic appeal of the text. In the Books of the Dead texts and vignettes do not always coincide for reasons of space.

The tradition of illustrations in Egypt dates from what we call the Dramatic Ramesseum papyrus. On the occasion of Sesostris I's accession to the throne a ceremonial play was written and, in all likelihood, performed. Thirty illustrations were added to the text to emphasize the most important moments in the play. They form a "mnemo-technical aid to the text". This sequence of scenes is considered to be the oldest surviving pictorial manuscript in the world.

In the New Kingdom illustrations were again added, as can be seen in the great Harris Papyrus in the British Museum. Ramesses IV refers to endowments and the deeds of his father Ramesses III. Three vignettes show the pharaoh in the presence of the gods of Thebes, Heliopolis and Memphis.

Illustrated manuscripts are also found in the field of science. Mathematical manuals with collections of exercises and calculation tables are datable to the New Kingdom, even though the fund of scientific knowledge they contain is considerably older. The illustrations inserted into the texts are of value scientifically, and they explain the corresponding exercise or calculation. Instructions for the building of a vault which are comparable to architectural drawings can be traced to the Third Dynasty. The first map of the world that has come down to us likewise served a practical purpose. It was produced in the Twentieth Dynasty and marks the position of quarries suitable for mining in Wadi Hammama together with their access roads. Marginal notes written in the cursive hieroglyphic script known as hieratic serve as orientation guides. Different colours on the map indicate various kinds of rock. This papyrus is now in the Egyptian Museum in Turin.

In the same collection there is a unique work which is well known among experts as the "erotic Turin papyrus" but was not published in its complete form until 1973. In this work, dating from the Twentieth Dynasty, an elderly man's sexual escapades with prostitutes are recounted.

What is shown in the pictures is explained by marginal notes, which are difficult to decipher. This papyrus also includes a sequence of scenes of satirical content, similar to those on ostraca. They include fairy-tales and animal fables in comic strip form. There is one picture with hippopotami sitting on trees and swallows that cannot fly and an animal orchestra caricaturing, both in their posture and in their equipment, the ladies' orchestras often found on mural pictures. The Egyptian fables may be forgotten myths. Unfortunately it is impossible, in most cases, to trace their literary origin. Literary texts were never illustrated, or at least, none have ever been found. Those literary manuscripts that have survived are often academic exercises and were only rarely intended for bibliophils. It appears that a story was told either in words or in pictures.

This conclusion suggests itself particularly when reflecting on the motifs used in pictorial stories on papyri and ostraca. Animal motifs are predominant. Fables, whether based on myth or original creations, seem to have been particularly popular. They were passed on only in pictures, not in texts. A collection of ostraca with animal motifs probably served as illustrations for a fairy-story teller when telling his tale to his mostly illiterate listeners. The origins of European fables precede Aesop and go back to the early Egyptians. Their themes are not found in official tomb or temple art.

Literature referring to the Other World (already mentioned at the beginning of this section) forms a special category in early Egyptian book illustration. It developed in very diverse forms out of the pyramid texts created for royal funerals. At first, these were recorded in the burial chambers and the corridors leading to them inside the pyramids of the kings of the Fifth Dynasty, appearing for the first time in the pyramid of Unas around 2300 BC. During the First Intermediate Period a change came about in the funeral practices for people who were not of royal blood. This gave rise to the appearance of the so-called "coffin texts", which were religious texts recorded on the outsides and lids of some coffins. It was not, however, until the New Kingdom that these texts became an apparently essential element in the tomb furnishings of well-to-do people. Here they appeared in a book form which was typical of Ancient Egypt, the papyrus roll. This was usually inserted into the hollow body of a statue of the god Osiris-Sokaris or between the mummy's bandages inside the coffin. The texts, which were intended to accompany the dead person's voyage to the Other World and his stay there, were passed on in the form of aphorisms and were often edited. At present, we have information on 193 aphorisms. The texts were written in black script. Headings and accentuated sections were done in red. Illustrations and vignettes were placed, as already mentioned, in the midst of the text. The manner of execution varied according to the period. Illustrations of the Eighteenth Dynasty appear as gaily-coloured pictures and line drawings. Pictures in the Books of the Dead of the Twenty-first Dynasty are particularly effective, stylistically refined and generally extremely accomplished in their design and composition, technical mastery and use of abstraction (see Plates 56—59, the Book of the Dead of Cheritwebeshet). In this and other examples of literature of the time about the Other World we can clearly see the freedom which the illustrator was able to exploit. Although the rules governing the use of pictorial motifs were firmly established, the artist was nevertheless free to contribute new ways of seeing, as in the portrayal of faces and bodies. He could also apply different techniques within the same illustration. Thus, for instance, the painted vignette in chapter 42 of the Book of the Dead of Cheritwebeshet (Plate 56) can be contrasted with the almost graphically conceived section in Plate 59. Some vignettes have not yet been interpreted.

Illustrations in literature concerned with the Other World are stylistically closely linked to mural painting. However, as a result of their difference in size and in the material on which they are painted (papyrus as opposed to wall plaster), the literary scenes reveal a technically finer execution, an apparently lighter and softer brushwork. The method of working was as follows. First, the draughtsman executed the corresponding illustrations in red on the papyrus roll according to the overall conception given to him. If necessary, they were then corrected in black and finally completed in colour by the painter. The colours harmonized with the background colour of the design, in accordance with the accepted convention also followed in larger, single-plane mural paintings. The script-painter, or scribe, then inserted the texts in the spaces left for them.

Papyrus, a very absorbent, flexible and whitish writing-material, was not only in great demand throughout the country — and was, therefore, precious — it was also exported to Syria and the Aegean. The word papyrus probably derives from the term "pa-puro", meaning "that of the pharaoh". From this it can be concluded that papyrus, "that of the pharaoh", was also a royal, state monopoly. The manufacturing process was known by about 3000 BC and it followed several stages. The fibrous pulp from the green stems of the papyrus plant (*Cyperus papyrus*), which grew in dense stands along the banks of the Nile and could reach 6 m high and become as thick as an arm, was first cut into strips of equal size. A layer of strips was then spread out, with another layer crosswise on top of it. When both layers had been sprayed with water, they were placed between two cloths and hammered into one another with a wooden mallet. The final stage consisted of compressing and polishing the sheets. There were two sorts of papyrus. The better one was made from broad strips from the inner parts of the pulpy stem in the same manner as described above.

Sheets of papyrus made during the New Kingdom measured up to 42 cm in length and up to 48 cm in width. Rolls were made by sticking the sheets together. In the New Kingdom a roll generally consisted of twenty sheets. The longest papyrus still in existence, an economic text, is about 40 m long.

When working on a papyrus, a painter or scribe squatted on a mat with his legs crossed beneath him and held the roll on his knees. He first completed the front page, which had horizontal fibres, and then rolled it inwards. Impressive figures representing these clever and creative men have come down to us in the so-called statues of scribes.

CHRONOLOGICAL TABLE

Before 5000 BC	Paleolithic period
5000—4000 BC	Neolithic period Lower Egypt: Cultures of Merimde-Beni, Salame, El Omari, Faiyum Upper Egypt: Tasian culture
after 4000 BC	Chalcolithic period Upper Egypt: Badarian culture, Naqada I culture
after 3300 BC	All Egypt: Naqada II culture
2950—2660 BC	Proto-Dynastic period First and Second Dynasties: Egypt becomes a unified state. Features of a highly developed culture (religion, art, script, beginning of science)
2660—2134 BC	Old Kingdom
2660—2590 BC	Third Dynasty: Djoser and other kings; beginning of monumental constructions
2590—2470 BC	Fourth Dynasty: Sneferu, Cheops, Chephren, Mycerinus and so on; pyramids as royal tombs; Memphis becomes the residence of the kings; pyramids at Giza

2470—2320 BC	Fifth Dynasty: Userkaf, Sahure, Neferirkare, Nyuserre, Isesi, Unas; religious texts for the transfiguration of the dead pharaohs in the subterranean chambers of the Unas pyramid and those of the pharaohs who succeeded him ("Pyramid texts"); the sun-cult becomes the state religion; beginning of feudalism
2320—2160 BC	Sixth Dynasty: Teti, Pepi I and II, Merenre I and II, and so on; the claim by high officials for a share in the pharaoh's central power leads to the decline of the State
2160—2134 BC	Seventh and Eighth Dynasties
2134—2040 BC	First Intermediate Period
2040—1660 BC	Middle Kingdom
2040 BC	Re-unification of Egypt by Mentuhotpe II; Thebes becomes a residential city
2040—1991 BC	Eleventh Dynasty, second half (Thebes): Mentuhotpe II and III
1991—1785 BC	Twelfth Dynasty: Sesostris I—III, Ammenemes I—IV; the Faiyum swamps are turned into agricultural land; flourishing trade with the Sudan; new impetus in all fields of the arts (portrait heads of kings showing individual features, philosophical writings and works of fiction); later this period came to be thought of as the classical period; royal tombs in pyramid form
1785—c. 1660 BC	Thirteenth and Fourteenth Dynasties: numerous kings in rapid succession
c. 1660—1559 BC	Second Intermediate Period Fifteenth and Sixteenth Dynasties: Hyksos kings. The rule of the Asiatic Hyksos in the delta and Middle Egypt introduced the horse, carriages, and the working of bronze; the foreign rulers were driven out by a prince of Upper Egypt (Kamose) Seventeenth Dynasty: Kings of Upper Egypt (Thebes)
1559—1085 BC	New Kingdom
1559—1378 BC	Eighteenth Dynasty: Amosis, Amenophis I, Tuthmosis I and II, Queen Hatshepsut. Tuthmosis III, IV, Amenophis III; Egypt, now a world power, extends from the Fifth Cataract of the Nile to the Euphrates; royal tombs in the Valley of the Kings in Thebes-West; art flourishes; Amon of Karnak becomes main god of the kingdom; feverish building activity; enforced tribute brings refinement of customs (the affluent society)
1378—1362 BC	Pharaoh Akhenaten and Queen Nefertiti sever links with the priesthood of Amon of Thebes; the pharaoh introduces a new ideology, the religion of the Aten, personified in the sun-disc; the pharaoh is the most fervent propagator of new ideas; naturalistic traits in the arts; royal residence is moved to El-Amarna (Amarna period); loss of Egypt's possessions in Asia; after the pharaoh's death the former conditions began to be restored. Successors: Smenkhkare, Tutankhamen, Ay, Horemhab
1320—1200 BC	Nineteenth Dynasty: Sethos I, Ramesses II, Merneptah, Sethos II, and so on; political power moved to Lower Egypt; building activity; Egypt regains its supremacy in Palestine; wars with the Hittites; vast constructions in Egypt (Thebes) and Nubia (Abu Simbel)
1200—1085 BC	Twentieth Dynasty: Ramesses III—XI; under Ramesses III victory over the Lybians and tribes of the eastern Mediterranean lands; then

	decline of the empire; looting in the royal tombs at Thebes; corruption flourishes
1085—735 BC	Third Intermediate Period
1085—950 BC	Twenty-first Dynasty: division of the land: Lower Egypt with Tanis as residence is ruled by the royal kings; in Upper Egypt the priest-kings of Thebes set up a "divine state of Amon"
950—730 BC	Twenty-second and Twenty-third Dynasties: Sheshank, Osorkon, Takelothis; kings of Libyan descent, soldier-kings; residence remains in the Delta
730—332 BC	Later Period
730—715 BC	Twenty-fourth Dynasty
715—656 BC	Twenty-fifth Dynasty: Kashta, Piankhi, and so on; Cushitic kings conquer Egypt; worship of Amon; the function of "the Wife of the God Amon" becomes important in religion and in politics
664—525 BC	Twenty-sixth Dynasty: Sais becomes royal residence; Saite Period, pharaohs by the names of Psammetichus I, Necho, Apries, Amasis, and so on; renaissance of the arts, modelled on the Middle Kingdom; bronze as material for sculpture
525—404 BC	Twenty-seventh Dynasty: First Persian Period — Cambyses, Darius, Xerxes
404—341 BC	Twenty-eighth to Thirtieth Dynasties: Nectanebes I—II; brief recovery of Egyptian control
341—332 BC	Thirty-first Dynasty: Second Persian Period; Alexander the Great conquers Egypt in his battles against the Persians
305—30 BC	Ptolemaic rule, the successors of Alexander's Macedonian generals (Ptolemy I—XV, Cleopatra VII); they slowly became pharaohs; the result is a mixed culture; vast building activity in Upper Egypt (Edfu, Kom Ombo, Esna); corruption and murder among the members of the dynasty
30 BC	Egypt becomes part of the Roman Empire

SELECT BIBLIOGRAPHY

1 General Books
H. SCHÄFER, *Von ägyptischer Kunst, besonders der Zeichenkunst*, Revised by E. Brunner-Traut, Wiesbaden, 1963
W. WOLF, *Die Kunst Ägyptens*, Stuttgart, 1957
H. W. MÜLLER, *Altägyptische Malerei*, Berlin, 1959
N. DAVIES, *Ancient Egyptian Paintings III*, Text, Chicago, 1936
CLAUDE VANDERLEYEN and others, *Das alte Ägypten*, Berlin, 1975
Propyläen-Kunstgeschichte, vol. 15

2 Ostraca
G. DARESAY, "Ostraca" (25 001-25 385), *Catalogue Général du Musée du Caire*, Cairo, 1901
J. VANDIER-D'ABBADIE, *Catalogue des Ostraca Figurés de Deir el-Medinah*, Documents de fouilles, part II, Cairo, 1936—7

E. Brunner-Traut, *Die altägyptischen Scherbenbilder (Bildostraka) der deutschen Museen und Sammlungen*, Wiesbaden, 1956

R. Anthes, "Studienzeichnungen altägyptischer Maler", *Pantheon*, 9, 1939

E. Brunner-Traut, "Ägyptische Tiermärchen", *Zeitschrift für ägyptische Sprache und Altertumskunde*, 80, 1955, p. 12 ff.

R. Würfel, "Die ägyptische Fabel in Bild, Kunst und Literatur", *Wissenschaftliche Zeitschrift der Universität Leipzig*, 1952—3, vol. 2, p. 63

Bengt E. F. Peterson, *Zeichnungen aus einer Totenstadt*, Medelhavsmuseum Stockholm, Bull. 7—8, 1973

Lexikon der Ägyptologie, edited by Wolfgang Helck and Wolfhart Westendorf, Wiesbaden, 1981, Issue 24, Art. "Malerei", and Issue 28, Art. "Ostrakon", and all the included literature

3 Book Painting

M. Pieper, "Die altägyptische Buchmalerei, verglichen mit der griechischen und früh-mittelalterlichen", *Jahrbuch des Deutschen Archäologischen Institutes*, 48, 1933, p. 40 ff.

K. Sethe, "Dramatische Texte zu altägyptischen Mysterienspielen I and II: Der Dramatische Ramesseumspapyrus", *Untersuchung zur Geschichte und Altertumskunst Ägyptens*, 10, Leipzig, 1928

4 Working Methods

T. Anthes, "Werkverfahren ägyptischer Bildhauer", *Mitteilungen des deutschen Archäologischen Museums*, 10, No. 2, 1941

E. Iversen, *Canon and Proportion in Egyptian Art*, London, 1955

5 Problems of Colour

H. Kees, "Farbensymbolik in ägyptischen religiösen Texten", *Nachrichten der Akademie der Wissenschaften zu Göttingen*, phil.-hist. Klasse, 11, 1943

A. Lucas, *Ancient Egyptian Materials*, London, 1948

P. Reuterswärd, *Studien zur Polychromie der Plastik I. Ägypten*, Stockholm, 1958

S. Morenz, "Von der Rolle der Farbe im alten Ägypten", *Palette*, Basle, 1962

6 Problem of Artists

H. Junker, *Die gesellschaftliche Stellung des Künstlers im Alten Reich*, Vienna, 1959

W. Barta, "Das Selbstzeugnis eines altägyptischen Künstlers", *Ägyptologische Studien*, 22, Munich, 1970

7 Literature Dealing with the History of Religion

S. Morenz, *Ägyptische Religion*, Stuttgart, 1960

C. Maystre and A. Piankoff, "Le livre des portes", *Mémoires de l'Institut Français du Caire*, vol. 74, Cairo, 1939—45

E. Hornung, "Das Amduat", *Ägyptische Abhandlungen*, 7, 1963

The texts from the Books of the Dead quoted in the catalogue are taken from: *Urkunden zur Religion des alten Ägypten*, translated by G. Roeder, *Religiöse Stimmen der Völker*, Jena, 1923

Publication details of the papyri mentioned are given in the catalogue.

THE PLATES

1 Pottery Vessel from the New Kingdom
Leningrad: the Hermitage Museum

This picture presents a further example of painted pottery.
The vessel dates from the New Kingdom. Ornamental
and figurative decorations are spaced out over the body
of the jar in exceptionally good taste. The colours of the
delicate drawing stand out most effectively against the
light-brown clay. One shade of blue has survived particularly well. From that alone we can deduce that the vessel,
when produced, must have been painted in glowing colours.
This jar was used to hold offerings in a tomb and was also
used in everyday life. The material it is made from is prone
to evaporation and was therefore used to keep liquids, such
as water, beer or wine, cool.

**Pottery vessel from the New Kingdom
between 1559 and 1085 BC**

2 Painters' Sketchbooks and Pupils' Practice Books

Cairo: Inv. No. 25 002

H: 47 cm   W: 41 cm

This painting is technically of considerably higher quality. A pharaoh, again with helmet and diadem, is turning towards the right, his arm raised. The gesture made by his arms indicates that he is holding vessels during an act of sacrifice. Images of this type (for example, those in relief) show the pharaoh with an incense-burner in one hand and a receptacle for libations in the other, turning towards the god of the consummation of the ritual.

Here the lines on the surface were drawn with less haste. But this work reveals a different shortcoming: the student has not yet mastered the rules of proportion. The head is too small for the outspread arms, which are out of proportion to the rest of the body. They are too thin, entirely without muscles, and too long. The body lacks the harmony that makes Egyptian art so attractive to us today, in spite of its strange formal principles. In contrast to the body the head is almost Mannerist. It gives an impression of smoothness, and is well balanced. Here we can almost certainly detect the assistance given to the beginner by an experienced artist, as for instance in the far more delicate brush-strokes on the helmet and head. The drawing is done in red and black. The illustration shows only a section of the full-length figure of the pharaoh. It was found in the tomb of Ramesses VI. The scale of the drawing is remarkable. An example of this kind makes one wonder at how much diligence was needed by an artist, apart from his natural talent, if he was to acquire the technical know-how of his profession.

Standing pharaoh (detail)
drawing on limestone, c. 1120 BC

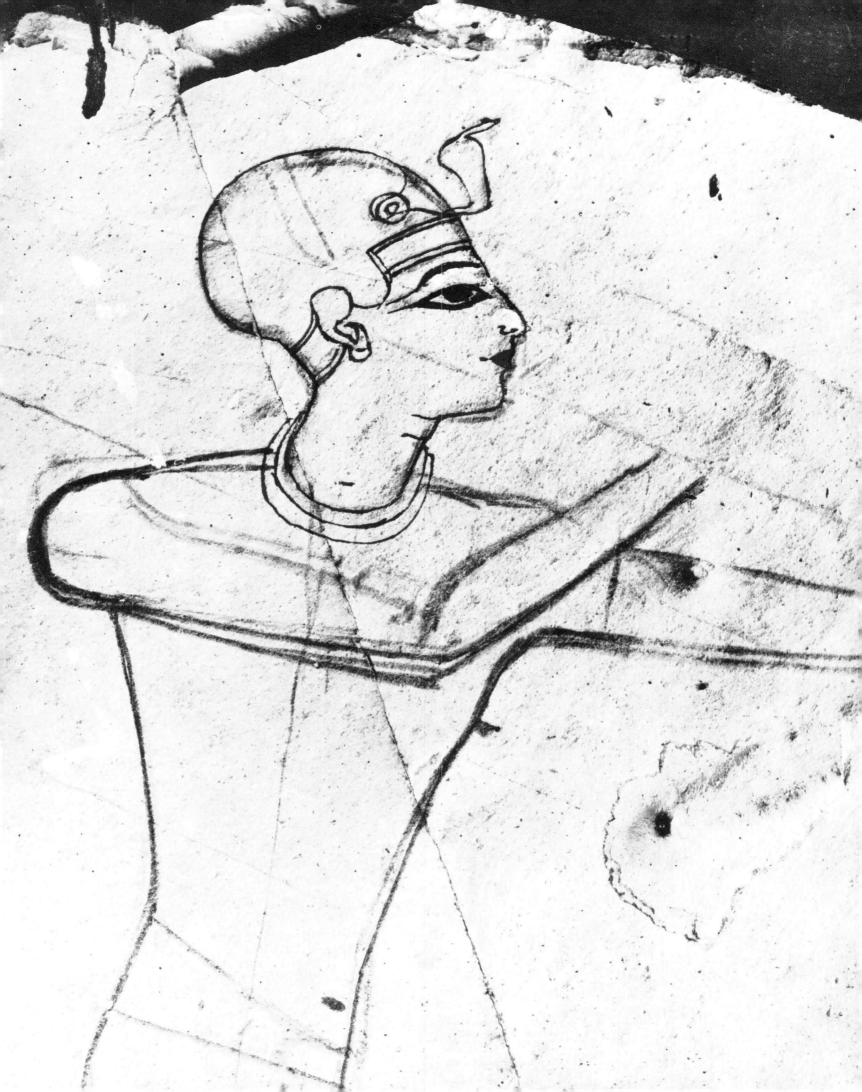

3 Painters' Sketchbooks and Pupils' Practice Books
Cairo: Inv. No. 25 132

This little picture gains in charm through the lively depiction of the wrestling scene. Two men in soldier's uniforms are wrestling, each trying to bring the other down. Probably the fight was taking place in the presence of the pharaoh. Similar scenes, though on a larger scale and executed in wall relief, can be found in the mortuary temple of Ramesses III at Medinet-Habu (Thebes-West). In this case an inscription underlines the sportive nature of the subject: "Behold, I let Thee tumble softly before the pharaoh." The text stretches along three sides of the picture.

The artist drew the scene on an area demarcated by two lines. These lines provide the floor for the wrestlers and cut off the scene at the top. At the same time they divide the lines of inscription from the actual drawing. Here, too, red and black were used for the original drawing and the corrections respectively. As far as we can see, the red line is slightly less sure. The black correction gives the bodies greater plasticity. Between the shoulder blades of the left-hand wrestler and the back of the right-hand one, an area of tension is built up by means of the thicker black lines. Since arms and legs are touching the impression is one of close contact.

The back of this piece of limestone contains an as yet unpublished sketch of two mice. The drawing of their fur is particularly interesting. This highly successful animal study must be considered a masterpiece.

Wrestling scene
drawing on limestone, c. 1120 BC

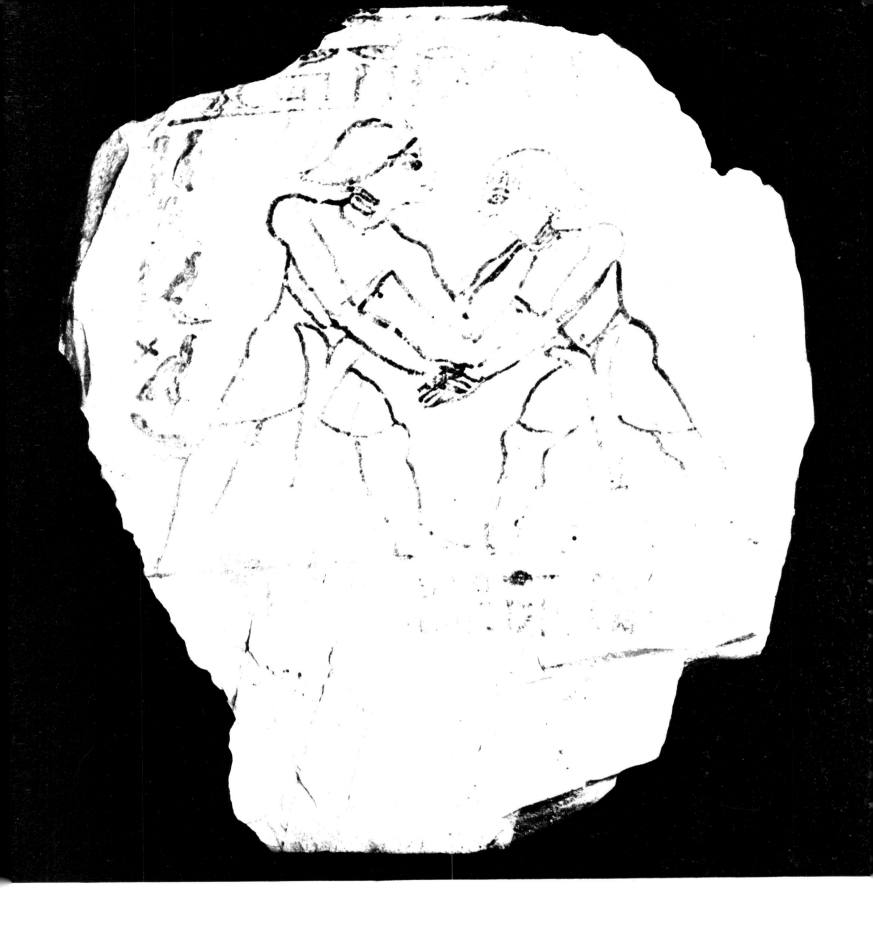

4 Painters' Sketchbooks and Pupils' Practice Books

Cairo: Inv. No. 25 125
H: 25 cm   W: 38 cm
Found in the tomb of Ramesses VI (tomb No. 9)

These two battle scenes are quite out of the ordinary. They are unusual since there is no other battle between a goddess (or a queen) and a king in high art. It is to be assumed that underlying this picture there are spiritual trends that are different from those that normally formed the background to battle scenes. The scenes of pharaohs' battles on the tall temple walls were meant to constitute monuments to the invincibility of the pharaohs of Egypt. They were visible from far away and influenced the thinking of the Egyptian people. Inside the temples the battle scenes are presented in a similar manner but reveal a slant towards magic and religion. It was the god who led the conquered enemies before the pharaoh and thus proved himself a master of history. Even inside the temples all battle scenes depict the invincibility of the Egyptians. Set as they are in the sacred premises, they document invincibility for all time.

The battle scene given here, on the other hand, depicts partners of equal rank. This points to a different sphere of art. Among the ostraca with pictures there are a large number with illustrations to fairy-tales, fables and myths, though most of the written sources are missing. The idea of a battle between a male and a female partner seems to have been incorporated into literature at a late date. This is perhaps a depiction of a story dated to AD 200, which describes a battle between an Egyptian named Pentuchons and the Queen of the Amazons. This would suggest that battles of this type were already known around 1200 BC, when this picture came into existence. An indication to this effect can be found in an item of contemporary literature, the Astarte story in the Amherst Papyrus (Pierpont Morgan Collection).

In the upper register of this drawing two chariot fighters stand facing one another. The left-hand part of the picture shows a goddess or a queen, standing on her battle chariot and dispatching arrows from an enormous bow. A charioteer has a firm grasp of the reins of the rearing horse. On the other side, the pose of the horse-team and the charioteer is identical, except that here a king is aiming the arrows. Only his loincloth with the royal insignia survives.

In the lower register foreigners are being hit by arrows. The figure who caused this slaughter has not survived, for a large part of the lower register has unfortunately broken off. To judge by the hair and beard the last of the foreigners to be hit seems to be a Semite.

The drawing is executed almost exclusively in red. The black of the final stage can be detected only in a few places.

Battle scene: deities and men
drawing on limestone, c. 1120 BC

5 Painters' Sketchbooks and Pupils' Practice Books
Cairo: Inv. No. J 65 429 A

This drawing of a cat guarding geese belongs to the world of fables and fairy-tales. We possess numerous pictures showing animal behaviour that runs counter to nature.

A cat, equipped like a shepherd with a bag hanging from a shepherd's crook, is guiding six geese with a whip. The running geese are divided up into two registers. In the upper half of the picture a nest with four large eggs in it can be seen. This nest stands outside the scene and probably does not form part of it. On the other hand, the juxtaposition of a picture of a cat as a shepherd of geese and a nest with eggs may have roused certain associations in the minds of the Egyptians. We do not yet know what these were.

Pastoral scenes had been very popular in large-scale art since the pictures painted in private tombs during the Old Kingdom. It can be conjectured that the shepherd's status or the repeated portrayal of pastoral scenes in fables is being caricatured here.

The drawing is most carefully executed and keeps to reddish-brown, yellow and black. The truthfulness of the details with which the artist has depicted the typical Egyptian tabby cat is remarkable.

Scene from a fable: a cat guarding geese drawing on limestone, c. 1120 BC

6 Painters' Sketchbooks and Pupils' Practice Books
Cairo: Inv. No. IAO 3005

Hunting scenes can frequently be found in tomb decorations from all periods. In the tomb they are of ritual character, apart from their documentary value. The hunt for wild beasts was essentially the privilege of the pharaohs. A certain special place was reserved for hunting the hippopotamus, which, during the Old Kingdom, was killed either by the pharaoh in person as his mythical enemy or in the presence of high-born dignitaries by their servants as a punishment for devastating the crops. During the New Kingdom the depiction of a direct confrontation between the hunter and the hippo was transferred to private individuals, whereby their hunt was raised to the status of a mythical event.

The sketch of a hunt given here is less conventional. Dogs are chasing desert creatures. Similar depictions can be found in the tombs of local princes from the early Middle Kingdom. An antelope, a lion and an ibex can be recognized. The dogs are attacking, while their prey are trying to escape or else, like the lion, are counter-attacking. This picture illustrates various emotions, such as the fear of the animals, the dogs' joy in attacking and the angry lion. One of the antelopes at the top is jumping on the back of a dog in fright.

This ostracon was obviously not the work of a beginner, for the flowing lines show great ability. Part of the figures in the middle have rubbed off. Red is once again used for the first design, and black for corrections.

Hunting scene
drawing on limestone, c. 1120 BC

7 Painters' Sketchbooks and Pupils' Practice Books
Cairo: Inv. No. 25 084
H: 39.5 cm   W: 31 cm
From the tomb of Ramesses VI (tomb No. 9)

This drawing of a hunting scene again derives from the rubbish-heap by the tomb of Ramesses VI. A dog is tearing a lion apart. The beast is trying to escape and its head is turned in fright. This drawing, again in red and black, is more elegant than the preceding ones.

It is uncertain whether this scene represents a hunt or whether it is something in the way of a caricature showing the insecurity of the position of the pharaoh, which was beginning at that time. For the lion is the symbol of the pharaoh's might. This idea had evolved at the beginning of Egyptian history and later sculptures of lions actually bore the names of the kings whose might they represented. This image is given most ingenious expression in the creation of the sphinx: the body of a lion and the head of a pharaoh with his insignia together embodied royal power.

Two groups of hieroglyphs in our picture name the title of the pharaoh as King of Upper and Lower Egypt. This suggests that this sketch was to be interpreted as a political caricature.

Caricature (?)
drawing on limestone, c. 1120 BC

The original image of the pharaoh as a lion encompasses the enemies he subdues as well. Here we have a Negro whom he holds from behind. The Negro's attire consists, among other things, of a loin-cloth decorated with strings of pearls. This red and black drawing reveals the hand of an experienced artist.

**The pharaoh as lion subdues the Nubians
drawing on limestone, c. 1120 BC**

For the workers on the necropolis and the temples, the
limestone with inscriptions possessed yet another function:
it gave them an opportunity to copy their eminent and
rich clients and fashion stelae with intercessions and thanks-
givings. This type of painted limestone fragment is often
of high aesthetic quality, because the methods used, the
feeling for form and the purity of execution represent real
craftsmanship.

This picture can be taken to be one of these substitute
stelae. The ram, the sacred animal of the god Amon, is
lying in front of a table of offerings. Sacrifices of various
types, such as loaves of bread and flowers, are piled up
in front of him, as on the stelae used in high art. The
drawing is adjusted to fit the shape of the stone. Unfortunately the piece is damaged. Two rows of inscriptions, one
horizontal, one vertical, in exceptionally beautiful script,
call the god Amon Ra and the benefactor of his little tablet
"the greatest among artists, Mechitepa".

**The sacred ram of Amon
drawing on limestone, c. 1120 BC**

10 Scene from the Tomb of Neferherpta
Early Fifth Dynasty
Saqquara

High officials of the Old Kingdom arranged to be buried in what are called *mastabas* (an Arabic word meaning "bank"), which lay in the immediate vicinity of the royal pyramid. The walls of these tombs were similarly adorned with scenes from everyday life. The two illustrations that follow are taken from the *mastaba* of Neferherpta. They are unusual in that they are only master-sketches, for the burial chamber they were intended to decorate was never completed. The painters alone had fulfilled their commission by doing the drawings. The completion of the design of the most important scenes made the premises "usable" in a ritual sense. Later, after sacrificial rites for the tomb owner were discontinued, the entrance to the cult chamber was restricted by the causeway up to the funerary temple of King Unas, and the *mastaba* was built over. So far few books on the subject have even suggested that it contains master-sketches made by an ancient Egyptian painter and is therefore something of an archaeological and artistic rarity.

These drawings served the sculptor as a pattern and a basis for his work. It was his job to remove the background and carve the figures out of the stone in three dimensions, as laid down in the drawings. Here the sculptor had only begun his work at the entrance to the chamber. Then, it appears, the work was abandoned. The reason for this, perhaps shortage of money or the sudden death of the client, cannot be established today.

What is striking in this painting of birds is the way they were painted. The feathers, both tail and wing, were outlined exceedingly carefully and the bodies of the birds are marked with dots. Such a sketch is useless for a sculptor. He could never engrave such fine lines and dots with his tools. Most of the hieroglyphic inscriptions are again finished, as on a mural painting. And they are equally carefully drawn. On the other hand, the men shown are, apart from their wigs, preserved only as sketches. Painted accessories are limited to the hair in the case of the human beings. A close analysis of what had originally been intended as patterns for a sculptor confirms the impression that this chamber was never properly completed and was merely made ready for use by painting it.

The figures of the working men are clearly freely drawn. There are no subsidiary constructions for the composition and proportions of the human body. The floor lines and the outlines of the cages were drawn accurately and, it seems, with a ruler. On the other hand, the hatching on the walls of the cages seems to have been added by a painter subsequently, for the reason just stated. The background to this picture is a smoothed limestone, which absorbs moisture rapidly. The skill of the artist is shown in the fact that a thickening of the lines as the result of an overwet brush or slow work is visible only in a few places.

Two colours predominate – red and black. The red was used by the first draughtsman; these lines were then corrected in black and drawn over. As we have seen, this is the normal method employed for paintings and reliefs. In this particular case the two colours have the additional function of achieving the effect of a painting.

The scene shows pigeons being caught. A number of bird cages are being filled by men, only one of whom can be seen fully in the picture. He is turning to his companion, who is coming from the right, a pigeon held in each hand. (He is not visible here.) The gesture of his left hand as it opens is explained by the hieroglyph "give". The man's lips are slightly apart and he seems to be talking. The birds, once caught, are locked into cages. Some are unable to fly because their wings are broken and are sitting on top of the boxes, which are covered with wire nets. Near the left foot of the man who is talking a rope can be seen fixed firmly into the ground. It leads to the clap-nets in which the birds are being caught. An explanation describes the scene as "The Bringing of Pigeons and their Placing in Boxes".

Catching birds in cages
master-sketch on stucco, c. 2500 BC

11 Scene from the tomb of Neferherpta
Early Fifth Dynasty
Saqquara

Here a flock of pigeons is shown as they descend on Neferherpta's fields. The birds are depicted in various stages
of flight and landing, and the density of the bodies in-
creases as they approach the imaginary ground.
This sensitive appreciation of the animal kingdom goes
back to the extensive religious changes which in the Fifth
Dynasty gave rise to the erection of Sun sanctuaries in
honour of the Sun-god Re. In them are scenes portraying
the harmonious life of men, animals and plants, created
and controlled by the god.

Birds in flight
master-sketch on stucco, c. 2500 BC

12 Scene from the Tomb of Pharaoh Tuthmosis III
(tomb No. 34)
Eighteenth Dynasty
The Valley of the Kings

This and the following pictures from the tomb of Tuthmosis III again have one unusual feature. This great general and politician among the pharaohs of Egypt had his tomb carved out of the great rock massif west of Thebes in conformity with the custom of his time. In this way the pharaohs hoped to provide for their dead bodies the security that was lacking in the tombs of the rulers who preceded them, most of whom were buried in buildings accessible to the public. The tombs of the pharaohs of the New Kingdom lie in a hollow valley in the mountains, now called Bîbân el-Mulûk, the Valley of the Kings. Each of these tombs consisted of a large number of rooms embellished with rich decorations. The entrance to each tomb was carefully hidden. The ornamentation of the burial-chamber of the kings was laid down at the beginning of the New Kingdom in a book of rituals created specially for the kings. Since the pharaoh's journey to the Other World had to be protected by magic, the texts now called the "Am-Duat", the "Book of the Gates" and the "Book of the Caves" dealt with the places and inhabitants of the Underworld. They also described all the dangers the pharaoh had to overcome in the Boat of Ra. These writings, generally known as "Books", frequently contain secret texts, the knowledge of which served the King in the Other World. The "Am-Duat" Book (The Book of the One Who is in the Underworld) can be found almost complete on the walls of the burial-chamber of Tuthmosis III. A purely external principle of division splits the "Duat" into the Twelve Hours of the Night, as well as into three registers. The artists have tried to transfer even the external appearance of a "book", or rather an Egyptian papyrus scroll, onto the walls of the tomb. The background is yellow, in imitation of papyrus. (The walls of the rock face had to be covered with a layer of plaster, since its brittleness would take neither relief nor painting.) On this plaster the texts of the "Duat" were written in Egyptian book-script or hieratic writing. Vignettes conforming with the external form of this book-script accompany the events and clarify them.

The depiction of demons from the Underworld among the scripts in the hidden chamber recalls the oldest type of illustrations. The figures are depicted simply in thick black outline. For graphic reasons the artists coloured in the heads. The movements of the figure behind the three mummified shapes are more impetuous than those normally found in relief or painting.

Figures from the Underworld: scene from the "Am-Duat" Book drawing on stucco, c. 1430 BC

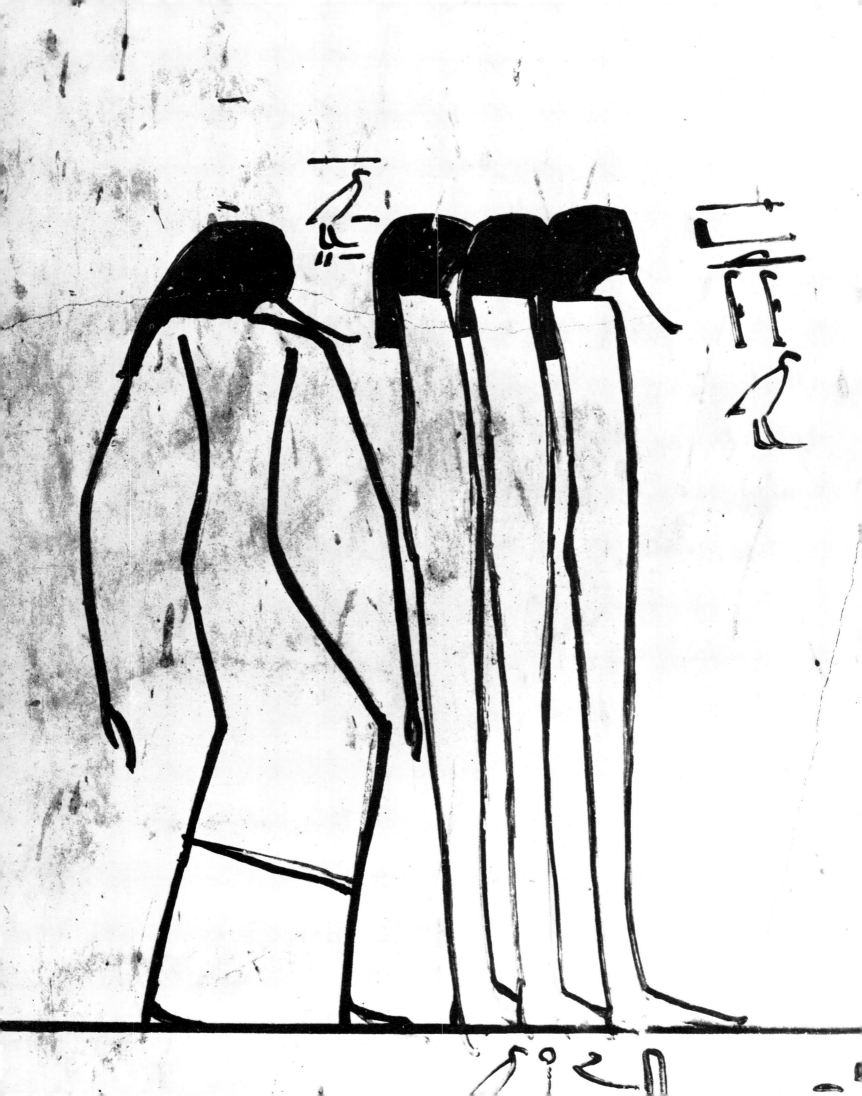

13 Scene from the Tomb of Tuthmosis III

(tomb No. 34)
Eighteenth Dynasty
The Valley of the Kings

On the east wall of the burial-chamber we can see an image of the Tenth Hour. The illustration comes from the lower register. Drowned men can be seen swimming in a broad river, but are barely visible in the schematically drawn lines of the water, for their bodies are given only in outline. The story of this Hour discusses a subject that must have been a source of constant concern in the Ancient Egyptian faith: can drowned men reach the State of Bliss even if their death was the result of an accident, and therefore did not have a natural cause? The Nile repeatedly drew down into its depths men who were working or bathing nearby. Even today drowning is one of the most common causes of unnatural death in Egypt. It can be assumed that then, as now, few people knew how to swim. Death in the water deprived the deceased of ritual burial, for to rescue the corpse must have been very difficult in those days in view of the large number of crocodiles in the Nile. Thus the dangers of the Other World overpowered the drowned person. This passage from the "Duat" tries to counteract this, for the drowned men are making their way by water direct to the Underworld and acquire there the magic protection that, on earth, would have been provided by a normal burial. Then they can join those of the dead who were transfigured by ritual.

The scene does not refer directly to the pharaoh but illustrates the important concept of the everlasting life enjoyed by drowned men in the Hereafter. By association this leads us to the pharaoh's journey through the Underworld. The drowned men, along with the Sun-Boat of Ra in which the king weathers the Hours of the Night, are floating on the Heavenly Ocean, the Nun. The beatification of the drowned people is carried out by Horus: "Ye who are the Ones who are in the Nun, the Drowned who Follow my Father (Osiris). May also Your Souls Live."

Horus here links the after-life of the drowned men with the myth of the death of his father Osiris. The corpse of Osiris was also retrieved from the Nile and endowed with life in the Other World. Thus the hopes of the dead for continued existence are bound up with the fate of Osiris.

Drowned men beatified:
scene from the "Am-Duat" Book
drawing on stucco, c. 1430 BC

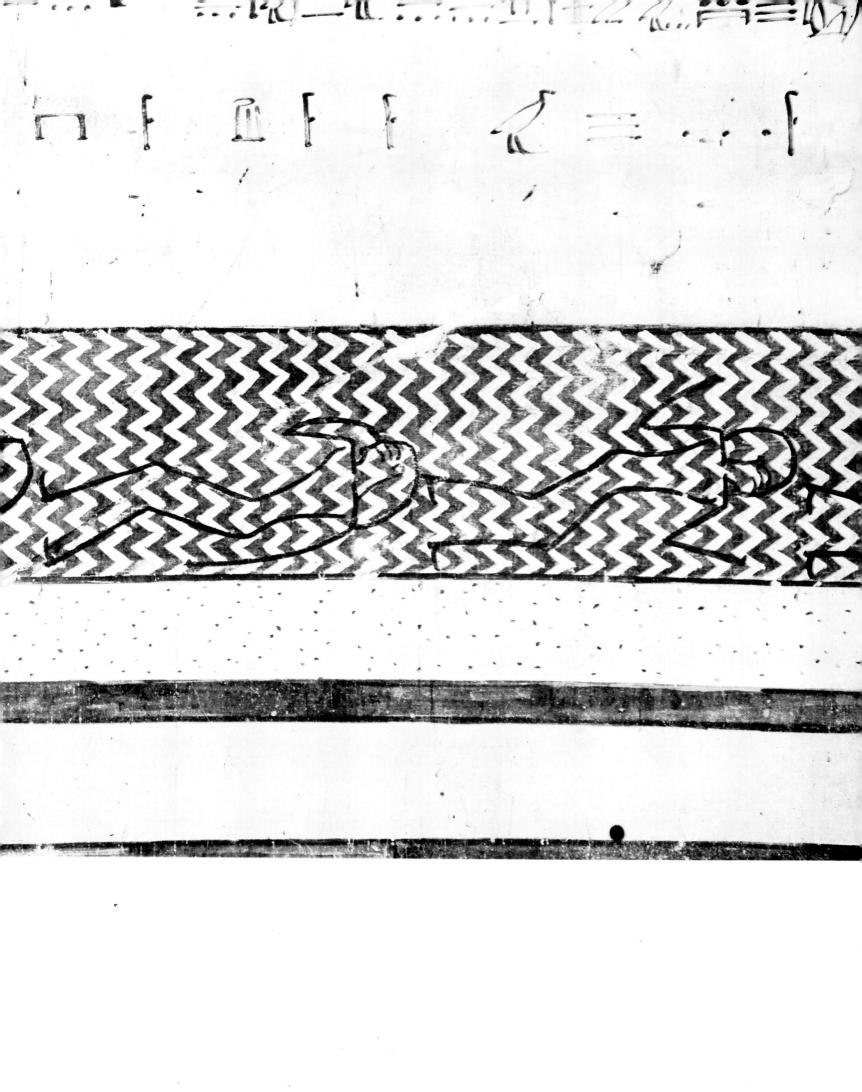

This picture of two soldiers behind a battle-chariot is again unfinished. Here, too, red drawing with black overpainting creates the atmosphere. The first soldier is busy at the chariot, his strikingly long limbs giving him an almost fragile impression. His companion, too, is clad in a loin-cloth and carries his sandals over his right arm. He enlivens the scene by his gait and the gesture of his arms raised in veneration. His left arm is elongated out of all pro-portion. An effective contrast is achieved by the leg mo-vement. The field of tension in this illustration runs along the line linking these two features. The lines of the bodies are soft. Unfortunately the contours of the faces are barely distinguishable, yet the chin and the somewhat effeminate chest of the first soldier and the softly modelled abdomen of the second would fit well into the period of Amarna art. The annotation on the upper edge of the pic-ture is composed of hasty hieroglyphs but is not yet given in the typical hieratic script.

Soldiers on a battle-chariot
master-sketch on stucco, c. 1360 BC

15 Scene from the Tomb of Horemhab

Eighteenth Dynasty
Sheikh Abd el-Gurna: Inv. No. 78, Thebes-West

Under Tuthmosis IV (1400 BC) the "Royal Scribe and Scribe of the Soldiers", Horemhab, had a tomb made for himself. An analysis of the style shows that another prominent member of the army, one Nebamun by name, had a tomb made by the same craftsman. Horemhab's tomb consists of two richly decorated chambers. The subject-matter of the pictures in the first chamber includes banqueting scenes, scenes of sacrifice, a scene depicting the levying of recruits, and a long procession of tribute-carriers before the pharaoh. In the second chamber the pictures turn primarily on the burial, but hunting and fishing are also mentioned.

Before we discuss this very charming picture of the mourners, which is only a master-sketch, a word on this professional group. The female mourners have their ritual model in Isis and Nephthys, who mourn by the bier the dismembered corpse of Osiris, which Isis has pieced together again. Female mourners were never absent from any standard Egyptian burial. They assumed the role of the mourning Isis and Nephthys for the deceased, who, according to ritual, had turned into Osiris. The mourners might well be labelled as a professional body, for they were as a rule hired by the bereaved for the funeral ceremony. We can gather from other pictures of these female mourners that they ruffled their hair, beat their bared breasts and uttered loud shrieks of lamentation. This manner of mourning the dead is still current today throughout the East.

Egyptian artists have depicted this act of mourning on numerous occasions, sometimes more expressively than others. This picture is once again a sketch and doubtless counts among the examples of restrained, though heartfelt, mourning. The women's movements are attuned to one another and are in full harmony. The style and taste of the time, which aimed to produce graceful effects in tomb decorations, has evidently exerted considerable influence on the artists who prepared this tomb. The women are alternately beating their heads with their right or left hands. They are squatting and touching the ground with their free hands. This gives an impression of restrained sorrow, which may have fitted in with the taste of the time, but does not provide such a clear image of mourning the dead. The lines of the master-sketch are haphazard and crude and even cross each other in parts. But it is the very absence of correction, as well as the thick brush-strokes and the smooth-flowing lines of hands, bodies and wigs, that make this picture so attractive.

The first design for the tomb paintings was carried out in the usual red watercolour paint on the plastered wall. The corrections, as can be seen, are unfinished. The first suggestion for the subsequent execution of the garments can be seen on the second mourner from the left. The slightly wavy lines do not only outline the body, they are also a first indication of the pleated garments worn at the time.

Scene with female mourners
master-sketch on stucco, c. 1400 BC

16 Scene from the Tomb of Horemhab
Eighteenth Dynasty
The Valley of the Kings

This illustration from the tomb of Horemhab presents an entirely different theme. The literature of the Other World, mentioned under Plate 12, includes what is known as the "Book of the Gates". The journey of the Sun-Boat of Ra, divided into sections and registers, is described here, too. In contrast to the "Duat", which describes places in the Other World, the "Book of the Gates" deals, in pictures and text, with the events outside the Gates that separate the Twelve Hours of the Night. The Gates themselves are relatively uniform in appearance.

Our picture is taken from the third section (the Third Hour). The events that take place in the region outside each Gate are somewhat mysterious. The God appears and gives the persons in the Underworld the opportunity to enjoy a continued existence by his very epiphany or manifestation.

This idea is contrasted with a highly materialistic approach. The God acknowledges their offerings from which they live or he grants these to them: "Eat ye your green Herbs, be ye content with your sacrificial Leaves, fill your Bellies, let your Hearts be satisfied."

A religion based on rites such as those of the Egyptians laid down rules for the behaviour of each person participating in the consummation of the ritual. The faithful make offerings to the God and he, in turn, offers a token of his grace. The corollary is that a sacrifice can force the God to bestow grace.

In these texts intended for the Other World the gods, to whom Ra grants continued life, must worship the great God in hymns: "Hail to Thee, Thou Great in Might. Glory to Thee, O Great One. The Nether World Obeys Thy Will."

The boat of the Sun-god is passing through a strongly fortified gate guarded by deities and fire-spitting serpents. Nine gods in mummy form are standing along the first wall which, like the second wall, is encircled with battlements. At each entrance and exit to the corridor between the walls there stands a guardian deity. Behind the fortifications a serpent is guarding the gate itself. All the gates are similar in construction and each has a name. This gate, taken from the second section of the Book of the Gates, is called the "Mistress of Nourishment". The gods in front of the outer ramparts bear the title "Third Ninthship of the Great God". The lower guardian, again in mummy form, is called, in conformity with his bearing: "Trembler of the Earth, Who Crosses his Arms before Ra".

The text along the side which is divided into two vertical bands by the serpent's tail reads: "She is at the Gate. She opens it for Ra. Reason (one of the God's companions) saith unto the Pricker (name of the serpent at the Gate): 'Open Thy Gate for Ra. Thou shalt Knock at Thy Underworld for the One who Cometh from the Horizon, for He Lighteth up the Entire Darkness and Maketh the Hidden Chamber Bright.' The Gate Closeth once the Great God steppeth within. Those who are at the Gate Hear the Closure of the Gate."

Some of the deities on the outer ramparts, as well as on parts of the ramparts themselves, are merely drawn. The red of the first drawing is clearly distinguishable from the black of the final version. The ramparts were first marked with a system of lines. The corrections by the teacher, who used a black paint, depart from the auxiliary lines, so that the upper part of the frieze is partly out of line. The designer had apparently made a mistake when he divided up the surface of the wall in order to fit in the deities along the ramparts. Some of the figures turned out too big. He would not have been able to fit nine gods of this size onto the surface of the wall at his disposal. He therefore had to divide up the space again and make the figures smaller. The big figures can still be seen beneath the sketches for the smaller ones. The sketched relief had already been partly carved out of the stone. The contours are handled with extreme delicacy and care.

Illustration of one of the gates and the ramparts of the Underworld: scene from the Book of the Gates master-sketch and relief, c. 1320 BC

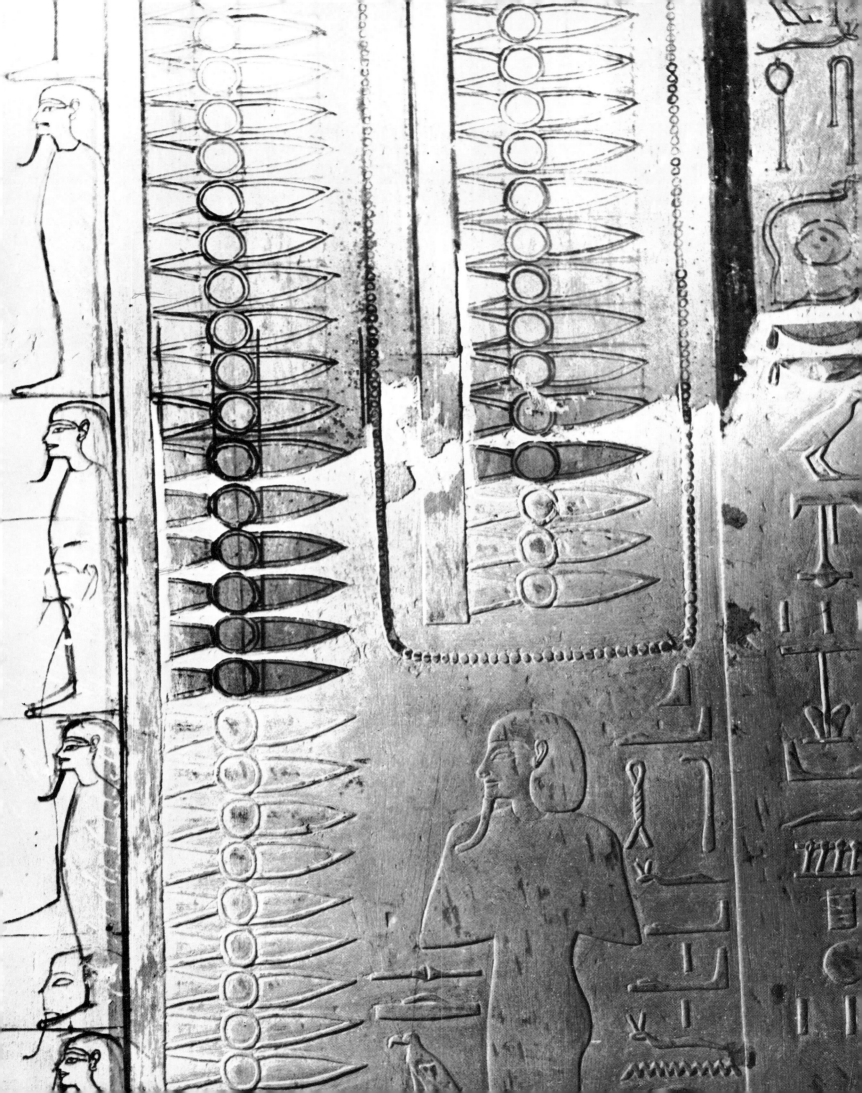

17 Scene from the Tomb of Horemhab
Eighteenth Dynasty
The Valley of the Kings

The boat of Ra is drawn through the Underworld by four deities. One of these gods, whose names are summarized in the term "Those of the Nether World", is visible on the right of the picture holding a rope tied to the boat. Ra, with the head of a ram and wearing the Sun-disc, is standing in a Naos. It is described as "Flesh of Ra". A serpent called Mehen is throwing its coils over the Naos. This serpent also plays a role in other books on the Underworld, for under its protection the aged Ra is transfigured into the youthful Sun-god who conquers the Realms of the Night by morning and appears over the horizon. His companions, the personification of Reason and Magic, stand one in front of and one at the back of the boat. The God is holding a sceptre in his left hand, while his right hand is clutching the symbol of life. A snake is rearing up in front of the sceptre, symbolizing "Prosperity". The boat of the God is cut by a line framing the middle register. Texts are crowded into the middle and lower register. They correspond in essence to the events outlined in Plate 16.

So much for the description of the scene. It clarifies the working methods used on a relief-covered wall better than many of the others. Texts and illustrations were laid out and drawn on the plaster. Here, too, the work of several artists can be distinguished. First there is the draughtsman, who used red paint; he divided the wall into sections and transferred the sketches from the papyrus onto it. The hieroglyphs, especially the squatting men, are in part drawn very cursorily. The draughtsman who followed him used black paint. With this he made corrections and improved the red contours, changing even the distances between individual figures and their shape. He was concerned with enabling the sculptor to do the engraving. The importance of the work of the second draughtsman can be seen in the figures in the boat. The first artist searched painstakingly for the correct proportions for the figure at the back, but they turned out too large in proportion to the main figure. The smallest figure, finalized by the black paint, did finally correspond to the idea of such a scene. It is brought into line with its companion figure, the personification of Reason. The auxiliary line, perhaps simply part of the original sub-division of the wall into squares, cuts across the neck of this figure. The hieroglyphs on the left, which act as marginal notes, become properly effective only in the decreased proportions. Certain parts of the Naos, the body of the God and the texts in the lower register have already been incised by the sculptor. The interior of the Naos was even given an (experimental) light-coloured coat of paint. The modelling of the body is very delicate and indicates a high standard of workmanship. The hieroglyphs in the lower register are again delicately incised. Individual letters reveal traces of under-drawing. It is noticeable that the letter "n" (a wavy line) was not always written out fully. In the last vertical line (on the left-hand side of the picture) the "n" is complete, but another in the same row was only shallowly carved out of the stone. In the first line on the right the block with the drawn letters was left untreated. The dividing lines running vertically, like those higher up, were also omitted here.

**The boat of the Sun-god on the trip through the Underworld:
scene from the Book of the Gates
master-sketch and relief, c. 1320 BC**

18 Scene from the Tomb of Horemhab
Eighteenth Dynasty
The Valley of the Kings

The scenes were taken from the second section. A part of the upper register as well as the important scenes in the middle register are given as details, out of their broader context. The upper register is formed by two groups of deities. One consists of twelve mummies. They are standing in their shrines with the doors open. A large fire-spitting serpent lies stretched out across the shrines. Four of the deities can be recognized in the picture, together with their open shrines. The first group of gods is followed by others who are emerging out of a lake, wearing white robes. The deities in the shrines are labelled the "Saints in the Underworld". The explanatory text runs: "The Divine Limbs Rest in their Shrines. Ra saith unto them: 'Open Ye Your Shrines so that My Rays may Drive off Your Darkness.'" The middle register shows Ra's boat meeting the earth-boat. The god's boat is known from Plate 17. It is drawn by four deities. The earth-boat is formed by a long staff with a bull's head attached at each end. On this staff sit seven deities, while two bulls stand at the front end and the back end of the staff. Eight deities are carrying the earth-boat on their shoulders. They are called "bearers". The seven deities sitting on the top are called "Those who are Swathed". The whole scene has the title: "This great god is drawn by the deities of the Nether Realms. Then this great god encounters the earth-boat, the boat of the gods."

The hieroglyphic text above the figures is a speech by Ra: "O ye gods, who bear the earth-boat, who uphold the boat of the Underworld. Let there be aid for your forms and let there be light in your boat, for that which is within is sacred. The earth-boat prepareth the way before me. The boat of the Nether Realms beareth my countenances. I traverse the secret Regions to take upon me the care for those who are within it. The earth quaketh, the earth trembleth.

"O Thee whose soul is revered. The double-bull is pleased. The god is satisfied with that which he has created." Thereupon the deities bearing the bull-headed boat of the earth reply: "Hail to Ra! May his soul be joyful with the earth-god."

The scenes are merely a master-sketch. But the shrines with the deities in the upper register are meticulously drawn and are partly painted. The bull visible in this picture was given details by the painter which the sculptor could hardly be expected to pay heed to. This leads to the assumption that here, as in the case of the incomplete burial-chamber of Neferherpta at Saqquara (Plate 10), the chamber was prepared for immediate use. The unexpected death of the king, or some other reason that we cannot now discover, led to the hasty completion of the work. Particularly interesting are the auxiliary lines that can be seen on the illustration. They helped the artist to transfer the mural picture from the papyrus to the wall surface. The individual phases of the master-sketch are in striking red and black tones.

**The earth-boat and its bearers:
scene from the Book of the Gates
master-sketch and relief, c. 1320 BC**

19 Detail from the tomb of Horemhab
Eighteenth Dynasty
The Valley of the Kings

Man's upper body, first design with corrections:
scene from the Book of the Gates
master-sketch and relief, c. 1320 BC

20 Scene from the Tomb of Horemhab
Eighteenth Dynasty
The Valley of the Kings

The illustration of these deities is taken from the same source, i.e. from the Book of the Gates. Particularly interesting is the juxtaposition of one drawn figure and one executed in relief. The sculptor clearly worked steadily over both figures and script, beginning from one side. We can understand that the division on the band of script that is outlined in the drawing could not be taken into consideration under such circumstances. The auxiliary lines that the painter used as aids in achieving the correct proportions are again of interest.

**Deities from the Book of the Gates
master-sketch and relief, c. 1320 BC**

21 The Book of the Dead of Neferrenpet

Nineteenth Dynasty (from Thebes)
Musées Royaux du Cinquantenaire, Brussels: E.5043
H: 23 cm

Published by L. Speleers, *Le Papyrus de Neferrenpet. Un Livre des Morts de la XVIIIe Dynastie aux Musées Royaux du Cinquantenaire à Bruxelles*, Brussels, 1917

Vignette of chapter 92 of the Book of the Dead.
"Spell for the opening of the tomb for the soul and the shadow of the unknown so that he may go into the day and may have control of his feet."
The custom of placing scrolls with collections of spells into the dead person's grave is known from the Eighteenth Dynasty onwards. Individual samples differ in length and composition of texts. Certain inseparable units of such spells existed already in the Eighteenth Dynasty. These religious writings embody prayers and incantations. They are attuned for the dead person's use in the Other World. The texts are written in hieratic script. The vignettes illustrate numerous parts of the Book of the Dead. The spiritual origin of the Book of the Dead is to be sought in the burial texts conceived for private persons and in the pyramid texts set aside exclusively for the King.
The division into chapters is not of Old Egyptian origin; it was undertaken by an Egyptologist (Richard Lepsius). The shadow of the dead, an undifferentiated body, can be seen in the shrine on the right. His soul, with a human head and a bird's body, is descending upon him to resuscitate him. The term used here means "taking up abode". The dead can then walk off freely, as is shown by the figure on the left, which is portrayed with the complexion and dress of the living. The sign of life (in the left hand), the Osiris beard and the symbol of rank are an expression of his divine status.
The upper half is the decisive feature of the composition. A certain tension can be detected in the design of the dark colour. As usual in this type of literature, the limited space confronted the artist with problems of composition. As the scene takes place in the Underworld, the sun appears black.

**Body and soul re-united
papyrus, between 1320 and 1200 BC**

22 The Book of the Dead of Neferrenpet
Nineteenth Dynasty (from Thebes)
Musées Royaux du Cinquantenaire, Brussels: E. 5043
H: 23 cm

Published by L. Speleers, *Le Papyrus de Neferrenpet. Un Livre des Morts de la XVIIIe Dynastie aux Musées Royaux du Cinquantenaire à Bruxelles*, Brussels, 1917

Vignette of chapter 151 of the Book of the Dead.
"Spell for the opening of the tomb for the soul and the shadow of the unknown so that he may go out into the day and may have control of his feet."
This chapter refers in word and picture to the burial of the dead. The objects the dead requires for proper burial are shown. We can see Amset, who protects the viscera of the (mummified) dead, like his brothers Kebensenuf with the falcon head, Hapi with the baboon head and Duamutef with the head of a jackal. The heads of these "Children of Horus" can often be found on the lids of canopic jars. In front of Amset is a head-rest, below a Naos.

**Canopic jar and head-rest
papyrus, between 1320 and 1200 BC**

23 The Book of the Dead of Neferrenpet
Nineteenth Dynasty (from Thebes)
Musées Royaux du Cinquantenaire, Brussels: E. 5043
H: 23 cm

Published by L. Speleers, *Le Papyrus de Neferrenpet. Un Livre des Morts de la XVIIIe Dynastie aux Musées Royaux du Cinquantenaire à Bruxelles*, Brussels, 1917

Vignette of chapter 101 of the Book of the Dead.
"Spell for the opening of the tomb for the soul and the shadow of the unknown so that he may go out into the day and may have control of his feet."
The dead man wishes to weather the evil hours of the journey through the Realms of the Night without danger in the boat of the Sun-god Ra accompanied by the deities that form the God's retinue. The boat of Ra (see Plate 17) must be intact if it is to take him aboard. The spell runs accordingly: "Spell for the protection of the boat of Ra." An injunction recommends that the spell be written out and placed round the neck of the dead. This illustration shows various aspects of the cult of the dead and also demonstrates the ancient Egyptians' skill at building boats. These light sailing-boats were used on the Nile. They were a normal means of transport and were used by the owner of the tomb when he went crocodile-hunting or hippopotamus-hunting or on fishing expeditions. The crew of the ship would be made up of a team of rowers.
The hieroglyphic text is inscribed in hieratic script, the handwritten form of hieroglyphics. The black writing is the text of the spell.

The boat of the Sun-god
papyrus, between 1320 and 1200 BC

24 The Book of the Dead of Neferrenpet
Nineteenth Dynasty (from Thebes)
Musées Royaux du Cinquantenaire, Brussels: E. 5043
H: 23 cm

Published by L. Speleers, *Le Papyrus de Neferrenpet. Un Livre des Morts de la XVIIIe Dynastie aux Musées Royaux du Cinquantenaire à Bruxelles*, Brussels, 1917

Vignette of chapter 102 of the Book of the Dead.
"Spell for man's descent to the boat of Ra in the Underworld."
The dead man is standing worshipping the god Ra in his dawn appearance with the falcon's head. He is holding his heart in his hands as proof that he has committed no sins. This alone wins him Ra's blessing and grants him admission to the Hereafter. The dead Neferrenpet will hardly differ in appearance in the Other World from what he was on earth. He is therefore dressed in the fashionable garments of his time.

Dead man worshipping the Sun-god papyrus, between 1320 and 1200 BC

25 The Book of the Dead of Neferrenpet

Nineteenth Dynasty (from Thebes)
Musées Royaux du Cinquantenaire, Brussels: E. 5043
H: 23 cm

Published by L. Speleers, *Le Papyrus de Neferrenpet. Un Livre des Morts de la XVIIIe Dynastie aux Musées Royaux du Cinquantenaire à Bruxelles*, Brussels, 1917

Vignette of chapter 111 of the Book of the Dead.
This picture belongs to a cycle of spells describing the
"Realms of bliss, the fields of offerings in the Other
World": ("A thousand miles long and unspeakably broad,
without fishes, sandbanks and snakes.")
There the dead man will be eating, drinking, ploughing or
harvesting; he will satisfy his sexual desires; in other words,
he will continue his earthly life. These fields are the abode
of the gods, or rather souls, the spirits of Pe whom the
dead is duty-bound to worship, as in this picture, in order
to win their goodwill. The coiling serpent in the second
half of the picture gains in plasticity through the thickening of the upper line.

Prayer to the spirits of Pe
papyrus, between 1320 and 1200 BC

26 The Book of the Dead of Neferrenpet

Nineteenth Dynasty (from Thebes)
Musées Royaux de Cinquantenaire, Brussels: E. 5043
H: 23 cm

Published by L. Speleers, *Le Papyrus de Neferrenpet. Un Livre des Morts de la XVIIIe Dynastie aux Musées Royaux du Cinquantenaire à Bruxelles*, Brussels, 1917

Vignette of chapter 107 of the Book of the Dead.
"Spell for the going-in and coming-out through the Gate of the Westerlies with Ra's attendants and in order to become acquainted with the spirits of the west."
In the imagination of the Ancient Egyptians the Realm of the Dead lay to the west; for while the fertile land along the Nile offered all possibilities of life, in the west, in the desert, there lay the necropolis, the burial-places of the dead, the desert land served only in death. Thus in popular speech the concepts "west" and "westwards" became euphemisms for the Other World and its inhabitants.
One Ancient Egyptian scholar advised: "Beautify thy house in the west and embellish thy seat in the city of the dead." This spell was to guarantee the living person free movement. The dead person is praying for this to the falcon-headed Sun-god. The remaining objects in the picture, two sycamores with the sun-disc floating above, stand for the Gate to the West (the horizon where the Sun-god disappears).

Prayer to the Sun-god
papyrus, between 1320 and 1200 BC

27 The Book of the Dead of Neferrenpet
Nineteenth Dynasty (from Thebes)
Musées Royaux du Cinquantenaire, Brussels: E. 5043
H: 23 cm

Published by L. Speleers, *Le Papyrus de Neferrenpet. Un Livre des Morts de la XVIIIe Dynastie aux Musées Royaux du Cinquantenaire à Bruxelles*, Brussels, 1917

Vignette of chapter 116 of the Book of the Dead.
"Spell for the recognition of the spirits of Hermopolis."
The local god of this town (in Egyptian: Ashmunein) was
the ibis-headed god of wisdom, Thoth.
The method used by the artist to grade and differentiate
his colours is interesting. The three figures of deities are
to be thought of as sitting one beside the other and the
painter used gradations of colour as distinguishing marks
and to make each of the figures clearly visible.

**Prayer to the spirits of Hermopolis
papyrus, between 1320 and 1200 BC**

28 The Book of the Dead of Neferrenpet
Nineteenth Dynasty (from Thebes)
Musées Royaux du Cinquantenaire, Brussels: E. 5043
H: 23 cm

Published by L. Speleers, *Le Papyrus de Neferrenpet. Un Livre des Morts de la XVIIIe Dynastie aux Musées Royaux du Cinquantenaire à Bruxelles*, Brussels, 1917

Vignette of chapter 115 of the Book of the Dead.
"Spell for the ascent to Heaven and the intrusion into the Amhet and to recognize the spirits of Heliopolis."
Heliopolis, now to the north-east of Cairo, was the main centre where the Sun-god Ra was venerated. There, too, the "Souls" (or spirits) of Heliopolis were worshipped, in the shape of phoenixes. They were usually represented as a trinity.
This example offers proof of the outstanding quality of Ancient Egyptian book painting, for the drawing is most elegant. The artist achieved this by means of a field of tension between the beak that juts out into the text and the tail of the other bird which breaks up the imaginary frame of the picture, and by his varied treatment of the feathers on the birds' breasts. With all this he bequeathed to us a good example of artistic taste and of his personal skill. The text that is visible belongs to chapter 124 of the Book of the Dead, and its "spell for the descent to the judgment seat of Osiris".

Prayer to the spirits of Heliopolis
papyrus, between 1320 and 1200 BC

29 The Book of the Dead of Neferrenpet
Nineteenth Dynasty (from Thebes)
Musées Royaux du Cinquantenaire, Brussels: E. 5043
H: 23 cm

Published by Speleers, *Le Papyrus de Neferrenpet. Un Livre des Morts de la XVIIIᵉ Dynastie aux Musées Royaux du Cinquantenaire à Bruxelles*, Brussels, 1917

Vignette of chapter 130 of the Book of the Dead.
"Book of the eternal animation of the soul on the day of the descent of Ra and in order to pass the Realms of Fire." The dead man is again found in Ra's boat. The god is depicted in old age, with the head of a ram. The Realms of Fire can be seen to the right and the left of the boat. An interesting postscript to this spell recalls the firm purpose behind the text consummated with magic: "Speak of the boat of Ra, which is drawn in pure yellow colour... and thou shalt set (paint) before him (the Sun-god) a figure of the Blessed (the dead) and thou shalt draw an evening-boat to the west and a morning-boat to the east of him. Bread, beer and all good things shall be offered in sacrifice. He for whom this is accomplished his soul shall live in eternity, and he shall not die again in the Underworld."

Dead man in the boat of the Sun-god
papyrus, between 1320 and 1200 BC

30 The Book of the Dead of Neferrenpet
Nineteenth Dynasty (from Thebes)
Museés Royaux du Cinquantenaire, Brussels: E. 5043
H: 23 cm

Published by L. Speleers, *Le Papyrus de Neferrenpet. Un Livre des Morts de la XVIIIᵉ Dynastie aux Musées Royaux du Cinquantenaire à Bruxelles*, Brussels, 1917

Vignette of chapter 135 of the Book of the Dead.
"Another spell to be recited to the moon when he is young, on the first day of the month."
Here Neferrenpet and his wife are obeying this command. A postscript that was added to the spell at a later date reveals much of the knowledge and application of spells for the living: "He who knoweth this spell shall be gloriously blessed in the Underworld. He shall not die again and shall eat by the side of Osiris. He who knoweth it on the earth, shall be likened unto Thoth (the god of wisdom). He is revered by men and is not incumbent upon the pharaoh's mood of the moment... and lo, he is hale to a ripe old age."

Dead man and his wife at prayers papyrus, between 1320 and 1200 BC

31 The Book of the Dead of Neferrenpet
Nineteenth Dynasty (from Thebes)
Musées Royaux du Cinquantenaire, Brussels: E. 5043
H: 23 cm

Published by L. Speleers, *Le Papyrus de Neferrenpet. Un Livre des Morts de la XVIIIe Dynastie aux Musées Royaux du Cinquantenaire à Bruxelles*, Brussels, 1917

Vignette of chapter 136 B of the Book of the Dead.
"Spell for the journey in the great boat of Ra so as to pass the Realms of Fire."
While in chapter 130 (see Plate 29) two fires are visible, the Ra's boat has already passed one fire on its stern and its bow is now moving alongside the other. The dead person, a passenger on the Ra's boat, is interested in its remaining intact and is therefore reciting a prayer. To the right and left of the falcon-headed Ra the artist has added two "Eyes of Horus", symbols of the movement of the sun.

The boat of the Sun-god
papyrus, between 1320 and 1200 BC

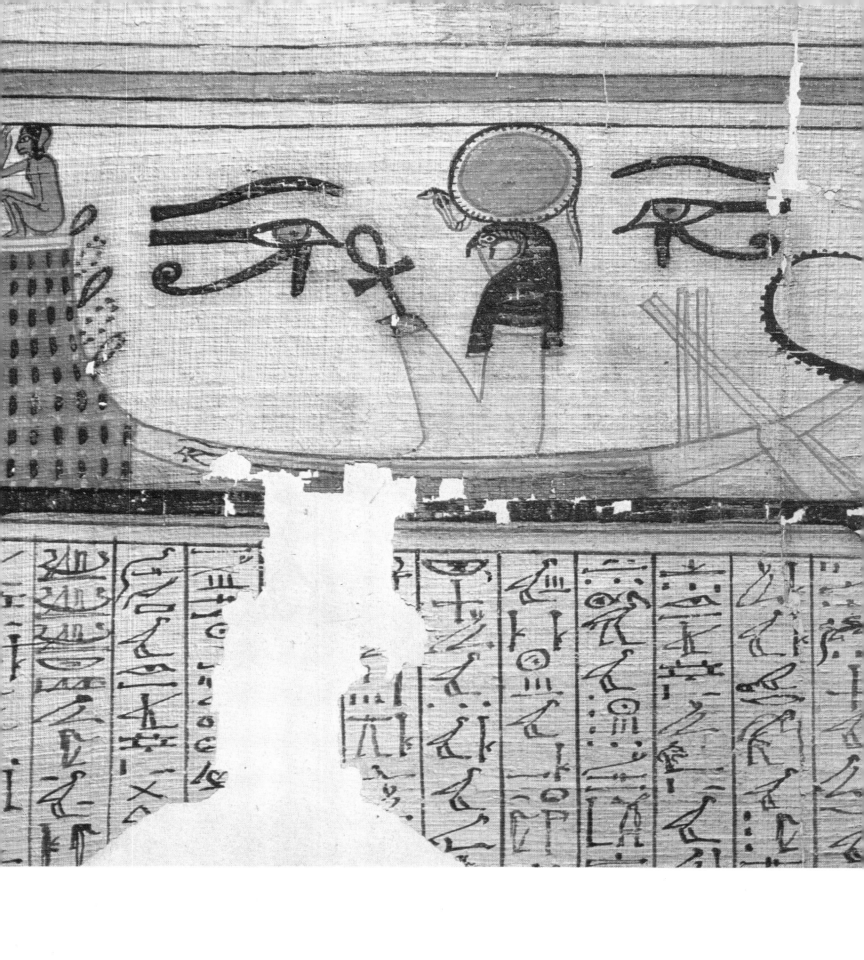

32 The Book of the Dead of Neferrenpet
Nineteenth Dynasty (from Thebes)
Musées Royaux du Cinquantenaire, Brussels: E. 5043
H: 23 cm

Published by L. Speleers, *Le Papyrus de Neferrenpet. Un Livre des Morts de la XVIIIe Dynastie aux Musées Royaux du Cinqantenaire à Bruxelles*, Brussels, 1917

Vignette of chapter 138 of the Book of the Dead.
"Spell for the admission of the dead to Abydos."
The dead man, in beautiful attire, is praying in front of Anubis, the dog-headed god of mummification. The back of the altar on which the deity is lying is formed by Osiris' fetish. Osiris is closely associated with Abydos and according to legend his tomb is situated there. The dead man, who yearns to experience death and resurrection on the pattern of Osiris, is similarly attracted by Abydos.

Dead man before Anubis
papyrus, between 1320 and 1200 BC

33 The Book of the Dead of Neferrenpet
Nineteenth Dynasty (from Thebes)
Musées Royaux du Cinquantenaire, Brussels: E. 5043
H: 23 cm

Published by L. Speleers, *Le Papyrus de Neferrenpet. Un Livre des Morts de la XVIIIe Dynastie aux Musées Royaux du Cinquantenaire à Bruxelles*, Brussels, 1917

Vignette of chapter 42 of the Book of the Dead.
"Spell for the prevention of having the eyes thrust out at Heracleopolis."
In this spell the dead man is entreating the gods who are hostile to him not to destroy his body. He identifies himself and individual parts of his body with deities: "My lips are Anubis, my teeth are Chephren, the nape of my neck is Isis, my neck is Neith, my phallus is Osiris, my belly is Sakhmet, etc. There is not a part of me that is devoid of a god."
The man at his prayers is painted directly into the text of the Book of the Dead. In comparison with the preceding illustrations, which were in the form of vignettes, this combination of text and picture offers something new.
This depiction of the dead has a special quality. It is not only most carefully drawn but it also stands out by its suggestive portraiture, as compared with other vignettes in this Book of the Dead. The artist has given the face a thoroughly lifelike touch, as for instance in the slightly drooping corners of the mouth and the wrinkles on the neck. The gesture of the arms and the twisted movement of the upper body lend the picture a certain grace. The wrinkled neck, the fleshy round arms and the soft body-lines, with the collar drawn in light perspective, impart a special aura. This papyrus holds yet another item of historical interest. Neferrenpet apparently bought the papyrus from a good manufacturer who had created a stock of Books of the Dead. His name has been inserted in five places only, while other spaces provided for a name remain blank.

Dead man praying for indestructibility of the body papyrus, between 1320 and 1200 BC

34 The Book of the Dead of Kenna

Nineteenth Dynasty (from Thebes)
Nederlandsches Museum van Oudheden te Leyden: Cat.
Leemans T. 2

Published by C. Leemans, *Aegyptische hiëroglyphische lijk-papyrus, T. 2 van het Nederlandsche Museum van Oudheden te Leyden*, Leyden, 1882

Vignette of chapter 1 of the Book of the Dead.
"Beginning of the spells for the going-out by day, the summons and the transfiguration (funeral) and for the ascent and descent, which take place in the Underworld. To be recited on the day the dead is put in his coffin."
A long procession of gift offerings and funeral guests stretches across the spell as an illustration of the long text. All the rites of a high-class funeral are depicted here. Similar scenes can be found in the tombs of officials of the New Kingdom. First in the procession come the servants, bearing gift offerings. The bulls are festively adorned and their horns are swathed. Several priests, recognizable by their shaven heads, are pulling the sledge carrying the bier of the dead. The coffin itself is standing on a boat for the journey through the Underworld. Isis and Nephthys, of whom only one is to be seen here, protect the coffin as, according to the myth, they protect the mortal frame of Osiris.
The Sem priest is walking in front of the sledge with the coffin. He is again recognizable by his shaven hair and by the leopard skin he is wearing. He is burning incense in his right hand, and is dispensing libations from a receptacle in his left hand. The water speeds up the movement of the sledge. Servants are carrying a second shrine with the god Anubis, the god of mummification. They are followed by the procession of mourners.
In this sequence of pictures the artist has again used certain methods to attain a succession of gradations. Similarly, the bodies depicted in a row are distinguished one from the other by different shades of colour.

Funeral procession
papyrus, between 1405 and 1367 BC

35 The Book of the Dead of Kenna

Nineteenth Dynasty (from Thebes)
Nederlandsches Museum van Oudheden te Leyden: Cat.
Leemans T. 2

Published by C. Leemans, *Aegyptische hiëroglyphische lijkpapyrus, T. 2 van het Nederlandsche Museum van Oudheden te Leyden*, Leyden, 1882

Explanatory text see Plate 34.

Funeral procession
papyrus, between 1405 and 1367 BC

36 The Book of the Dead of Kenna

Nineteenth Dynasty (from Thebes)
Nederlandsches Museum van Oudheden te Leyden: Cat.
Leemans T. 2

Published by C. Leemans, *Aegyptische hiëroglyphische lijk-papyrus, T. 2 van het Nederlandsche Museum van Oudheden te Leyden*, Leyden, 1882

Vignette of chapter 15 of the Book of the Dead.
"Veneration of Ra, as he rises on the eastern horizon of the sky."
In this spell the dead man joins deities in praying to the Sun-god. The morning, afternoon and evening appearance of the sun is sung of in hymns. For example, a prayer of the deities to the young Sun-god runs: "Hail to thee who riseth in the Nun (the ocean), who lightest up two lands (Egypt)... when he riseth mankind is jubilant and the people rejoice over him..."
Kenna and his wife, dressed in beautiful and fashionable garments, are lifting their arms in gestures of worship. The lady's pleated but diaphanous robe is drawn with great delicacy, while the tightly fitting loin-cloth of the somewhat stouter Kenna, despite his robustness, conveys great aesthetic charm. The face reveals the slightly decadent features of the period of Amenophis III. A feeling of liveliness is fully revealed in Plate 37, where Kenna is praying. The curly wig intensifies the impression of his robust build, for it is far from neat. Individual strands are tossed about the head in restless zig-zag lines. The raised hands have pointed, slightly Mannerist fingers, bent upwards. The fingers themselves seem to be in movement. The man's stout body is drawn in a line that varies in thickness, giving the impression of plasticity. This line broadens in places. This delicately drawn picture reveals the skill of the artist. No doubt, the craftsman who executed this Book of the Dead far exceeded the average standard of his fellow artisans.

Prayer to the Sun-god
papyrus, between 1405 and 1367 BC

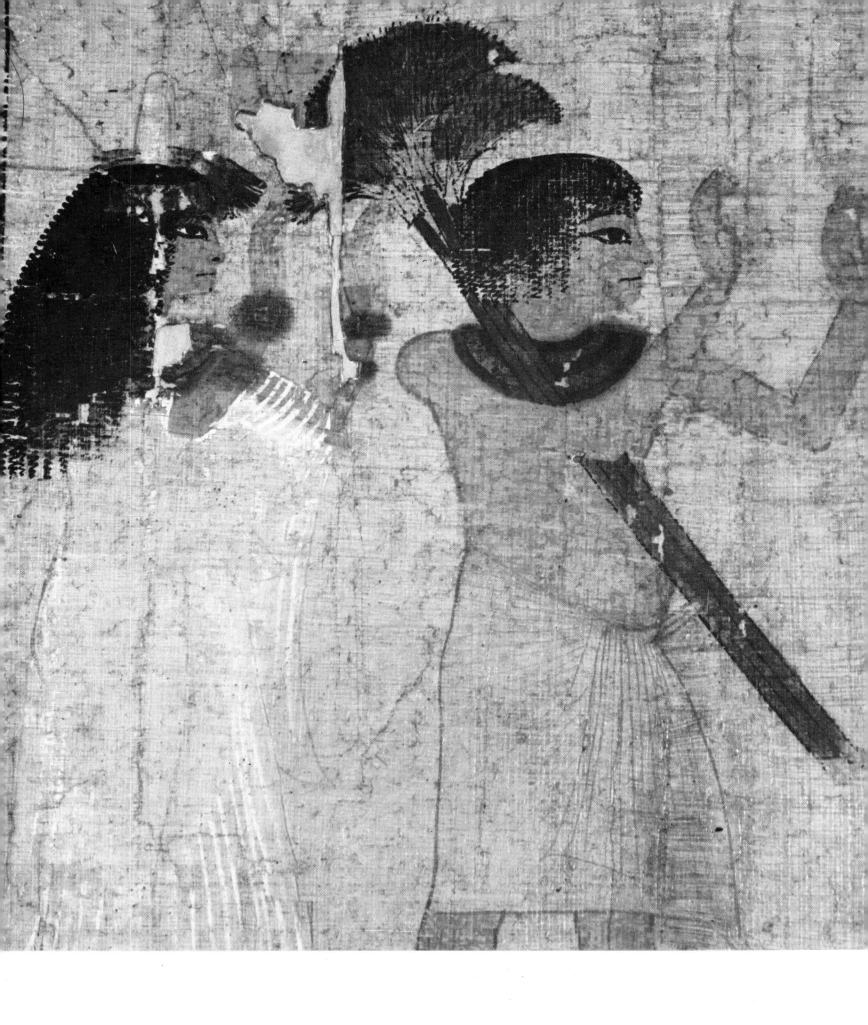

37 The Book of the Dead of Kenna
Nineteenth Dynasty (from Thebes)
Nederlandsches Museum van Oudheden te Leyden: Cat.
Leemans T. 2

Published by C. Leemans, *Aegyptische hiëroglyphische lijk-
papyrus, T. 2 van het Nederlandsche Museum van Oudheden te Leyden*, Leyden, 1882

Explanatory text see Plate 36.

Prayer to the Sun-god
papyrus, between 1405 and 1367 BC

38 The Book of the Dead of Kenna
Nineteenth Dynasty (from Thebes)
Nederlandsches Museum van Oudheden te Leyden: Cat.
Leemans T. 2

Published by C. Leemans, *Aegyptische hiëroglyphische lijk-papyrus, T. 2 van het Nederlandsche Museum van Oudheden te Leyden*, Leyden, 1882

Vignette of chapter 16 of the Book of the Dead.
This chapter comprises only vignettes for the sunrise and the sunset. Their charm results from their colour scheme.

The Sun-god rising and setting
papyrus, between 1405 and 1367 BC

39 The Book of the Dead of Kenna
Nineteenth Dynasty (from Thebes)
Nederlandsches Museum van Oudheden te Leyden: Cat.
Leemans T. 2

Published by C. Leemans, *Aegyptische hiëroglyphische lijk-papyrus, T. 2 van het Nederlandsche Museum van Oudheden te Leyden*, Leyden, 1882

These pictures demonstrate Egyptian ideas about the Day of Judgment in the Hall of Osiris. The scenes come from chapter 125 of the Book of the Dead, "Spell for the descent into the hall of the two righteousnesses". Here the dead man's behaviour in his past life is being judged. Here, too, a decision is made about his further existence in the Other World. The standard was set by fixed ethical norms. First a goddess leads the dead man into the Hall of Osiris. Osiris is the Supreme Judge and is assisted by forty-two assessors (see Plate V). Others present include Thoth, the god of wisdom, as well as Anubis, the god of mummification, and Isis and Nephthys, sisters of Osiris.

While in later Books of the Dead the entire scene in the Hall of Judgment is shown, here the individual phases of introduction, weighing and confession are turned into individual pictures. The confession, the "negative acknowledgement of sins", is, linguistically, placed in a central position in the text and reflects the dead man's major concern: "I have committed no sin. I have not robbed. I have not deceived. I have not stolen, nor killed anybody. I have not given short measure in bushels, have stolen no gift offerings, spoken no lies, committed no wantonness. I have not spoken foolishly, nor have I quarrelled with the pharaoh. I was not vain."

The composition is a random one and represents a shortened version of the constantly repeated phrases introduced by "I have not...". This "negative confession" follows upon an assurance of his sinlessness: "Behold I come before ye without sin or crime... I live by righteousness, I consume righteousness."

In Plate 39, Anubis is introducing the dead man. The dead Kenna is approaching his judge Osiris with a gesture indicating subservience (left hand over right shoulder).

The next two pictures, Plates 40 and 41 (detail of Plate 40), show him as he kneels in front of the table of offerings for Osiris, still maintaining this gesture of subservience. As in the preceding examples from this papyrus, the wisdom and grace in the representation of the man is striking. It looks as if in Plate 40 the painter was still slightly unsure of himself in drawing the right hand and the lower arm. He must have wanted to apply this graceful posture to the arm, which he does not seem to have succeeded in doing. We can sense the attempts he made to make the wrist and fingers more graceful.

In Plate 42 the scene of the weighing of the heart is presented according to an earlier conception. On the right, on an altar, Thoth is sitting in his baboon form. He is watching the weighing procedure on the larger than life-size balance with great attention. For on the scale-pans turned towards him there lies the heart of the dead man, which is being balanced against Maat, the proper way of life. The negative confession is intended to influence the process of weighing in favour of the dead man. For the Devourer, the crocodile-headed monster on the other side below the balance, is ready to devour the dead man's heart, should it be found wanting on the scales, thereby proving the dead man's guilt and cutting short his yearned-for existence in the Other World. If righteousness does not balance his heart and the dead man is delivered up to the Devourer, all that remains for him is an existence as a shadow, prone to all manner of punishment.

Anubis with the dead man before Osiris papyrus, between 1405 and 1367 BC

40 The Book of the Dead of Kenna
Nineteenth Dynasty (from Thebes)
Nederlandsches Museum van Oudheden te Leyden: Cat.
Leemans T. 2

Published by C. Leemans, *Aegyptische hiëroglyphische lijkpapyrus, T. 2 van het Nederlandsche Museum van Oudheden te Leyden*, Leyden, 1882

Explanatory text see Plate 39.

**The dead man before Osiris
papyrus, between 1405 and 1367 BC**

41 The Book of the Dead of Kenna
Nineteenth Dynasty (from Thebes)
Nederlandsches Museum van Oudheden te Leyden: Cat.
Leemans T. 2

Published by C. Leemans, *Aegyptische hiëroglyphische
lijkpapyrus, T. 2 van het Nederlandsche Museum van Oudheden te Leyden*, Leyden, 1882

Explanatory text see Plate 39.

**The dead man before Osiris
detail of Plate 40**

42 The Book of the Dead of Kenna
Nineteenth Dynasty (from Thebes)
Nederlandsches Museum van Oudheden te Leyden: Cat.
Leemans T. 2

Published by C. Leemans, *Aegyptische hiëroglyphische lijkpapyrus, T. 2 van het Nederlandsche Museum van Oudheden te Leyden*, Leyden, 1882

Explanatory text see Plate 39.

Weighing scene
papyrus, between 1405 and 1367 BC

43 The Book of the Dead of Pakerer

Nineteenth-Twentieth Dynasties (from Memphis)
Nederlandsches Museum van Oudheden te Leyden: Cat.
Leemans T. 4

Vignettes of chapter 1 of the Book of the Dead.
Like Plates 34 and 35 the pictures before us depict a funeral
procession. The event covers two registers.
In the upper register the female mourners have thrown
themselves across the path of the procession. The artist
has treated the features of mourning with great energy.
The faces are hastily drawn, particular emphasis being
placed on the elegant flow of the lines of the arms, garments
and the hair. In the lower register a team of oxen is visible;
it is being used to transport the coffin to the grave. The
swathed horns form part of the ceremony.
The burial procession in the upper register of Plate 43
continues in Plate 44. The dead man's mummy is lying
in a shrine, on the top of which Anubis, the god of mummification, is resting. A priest is walking in front, scat-
tering incense and pouring libations to provide for the
mummy on its long journey to the tomb. The mummy and
the shrine are being transported on a sledge drawn by
men. The one who is walking closest to it has his head
turned toward the god Anubis, thus creating tension
between himself and the god resting in majesty.
In the lower register, too, incense and libations are being
offered in front of a sledge-drawn coffin. Isis and Nephthys
are guarding the dead, standing on a boat-shaped sledge.

Funeral procession
papyrus, between 1320 and 1085 BC

44 The Book of the Dead of Pakerer
Nineteenth-Twentieth Dynasties (from Memphis)
Nederlandsches Museum van Oudheden te Leyden: Cat.
Leemans T. 4

Explanatory text see Plate 43.

Funeral procession
papyrus, between 1320 and 1085 BC

45 The Book of the Dead of Userhetmos
Nineteenth Dynasty
Cairo

Vignette of chapter 186 of the Book of the Dead.
This vignette is a continuation of Plate 46. Hathor, the goddess of love, or the goddess of death in Thebes-West, is emerging from the western hill. The collar *menat*, the symbol of the cult of the goddess of love, Hathor, adorns her neck. The stars on her body symbolize the function of Hathor as an ancient goddess of the heavens. The cow shape suggests that she is seen here as the death goddess of Thebes-West. The goddess's head ornaments are made up of two components: the crown of the goddess of love (the sun-disc with cow horns) and the feathers from the crown of the god of death, Osiris. Stelae can be seen on the lower part of the western hill from where the goddess is emerging. The lines indicate inscriptions that the dead man is to fill in, inscribing biographical details and his prayers.
The picturesque treatment of the flowers round the cow-shaped goddess is striking. The outlines are broadened (particularly those of the flowers). The stalks of the plants do not appear to have been drawn in outline.

Hathor, goddess of love and death, goddess of Thebes-West in cow shape papyrus, between 1320 and 1200 BC

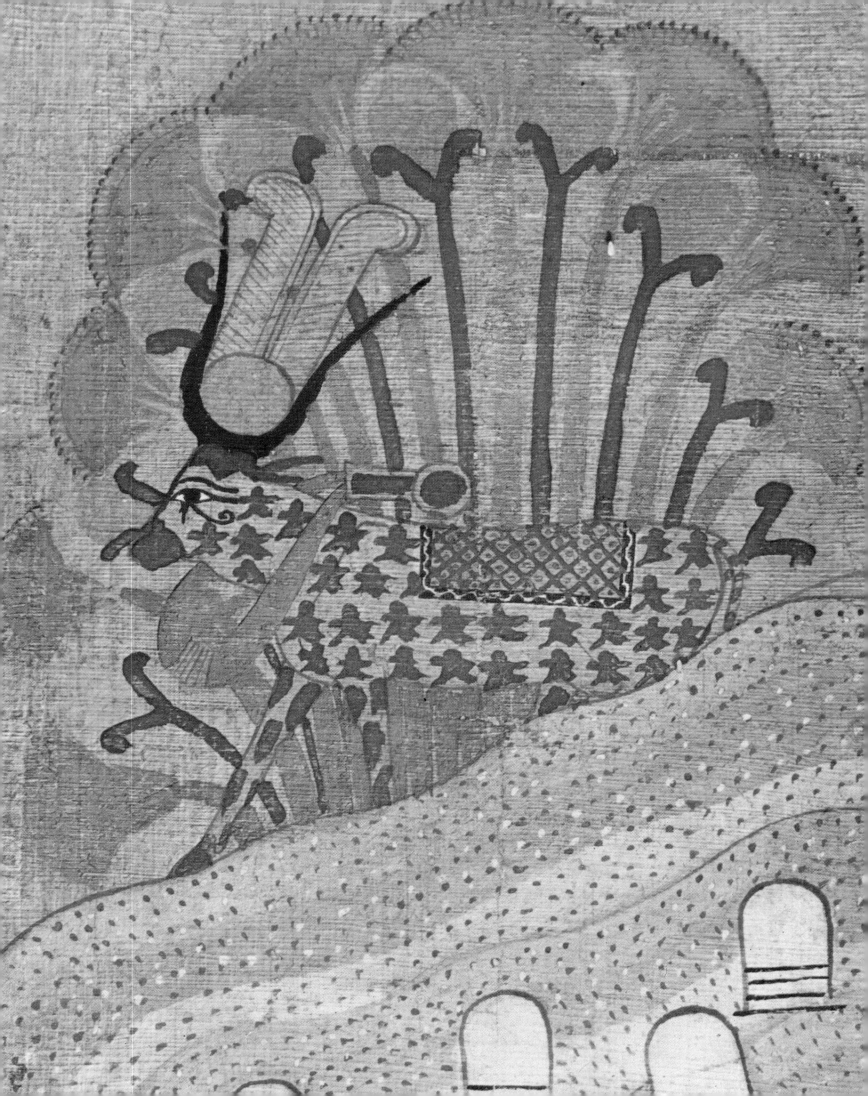

46 The Book of the Dead of Ra
Nineteenth Dynasty (from Memphis)
Nederlandsches Museum van Oudheden te Leyden: Cat
Leemans T. 5

Published by C. Leemans, *Aegyptische hiëroglyphische lijkpapyrus, T. 5 van het Nederlandsche Museum van Oudheden te Leyden*, Leyden, 1882

Vignette of chapter 186 of the Book of the Dead.
"Worship of Hathor, the Princess of the West, the Dead Man Kissing the Ground in front of the Mechweret-Cow."
The dead woman is praying to the goddess Toeris, who can speed up her rebirth. In life, too, the hippo-headed goddess has the task of assisting women in childbirth. In this picture she is standing on an altar with the cow following her (not visible in this picture).
In this illustration we can detect a clear departure from the trend of turning lines into planes, as demonstrated so impressively in the Book of the Dead of Kenna (see above). The graphic art of the period from which the Book of the Dead of Ra dates restored to the line its ancient function of delineating a contour. Slight touches, perhaps reminiscences of art from the time of the Book of the Dead of Kenna, leave vague traces of plasticity in the shaping of the arms and the flowing robes. The faultless execution proves that the artist had full technical mastery over his graphic media.

Prayer to Toeris
papyrus, between 1320 and 1200 BC

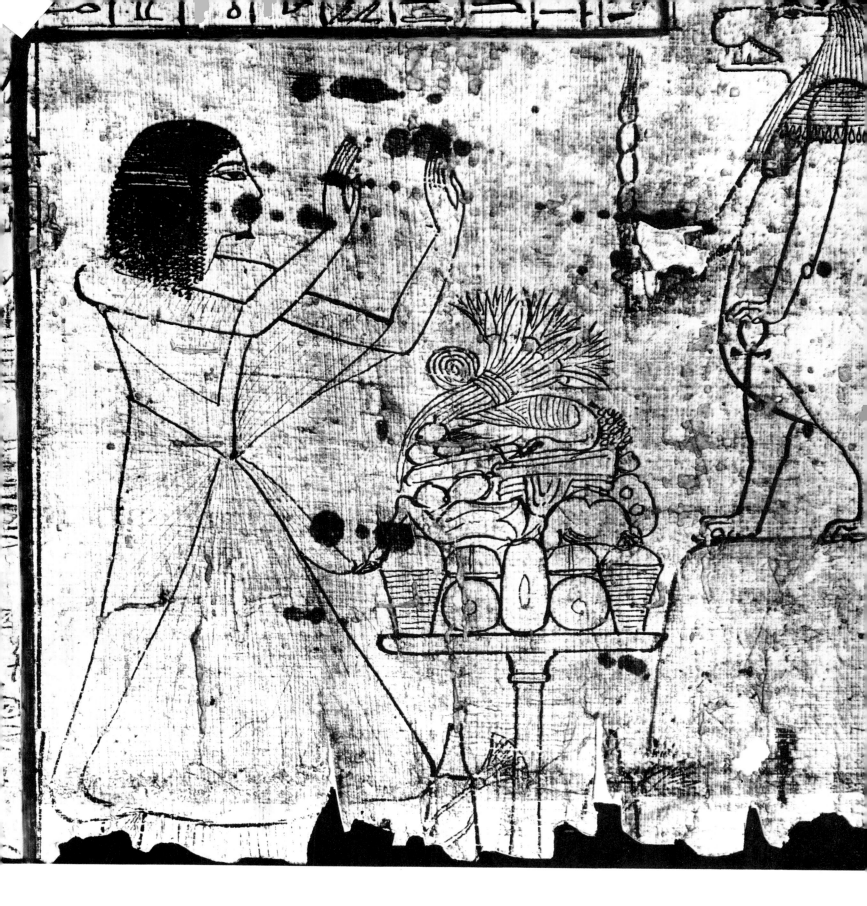

47 The Book of the Dead of the Lady Tashedchonsu

Twenty-first Dynasty
Cairo: Inv. Nos. 531 and 40 016
H: 275 cm   W: 28 cm

Published in: A. Piankoff, B. Rambova, *Egyptian Religious Texts and Representations, vol. III Mythological Papyri I/II*, New York, 1957
I p. 150; II Pap. No. 18

The Book of the Dead of Cheritwebeshet and that of Tashedchonsu belong to a category of literature on the Hereafter which cannot be classified as Guide to the Other World nor as Book of the Dead. While the content derives from the Book of the Dead, the manner of decoration corresponds more to the Guides to the Other World. These papyri are called "mythological papyri". In function they served as Books of the Dead.
Once again the owner of the Book of the Dead was a lady who undoubtedly enjoyed high esteem in society. She was a singer of Amon and a priestess of various deities.
The scene is taken from her Book of the Dead. It is complicated, as it seems that various elements from the literature on the after-life were being worked out for the pharaoh. Osiris is not represented in his usual form as a mummy. His composite shape (okapi head?) is modelled on the royal literature of the dead. In this picture Osiris is sitting on a throne and is turning towards the spectator. This removes the figure from its setting. He holds the symbol of diversity, a lizard. In front of him is Anubis' ensign and a Ba-bird, which represents a certain psychic aspect in the Egyptians' image of the soul. Behind it appear Isis (or the dead woman?) and Nephthys. The former is sacrificing a bunch of leeks.
This picture is restricted to black and white; the thicker lines again indicate plasticity.

**Scene with Osiris, Isis (?) and Nephthys
papyrus, between 1085 and 950 BC**

48 The Book of the Dead of the Lady Taucherit
Twenty-first Dynasty (from Thebes)
Nederlandsches Museum van Oudheden te Leyden: Cat.
Leemans T. 3

Published by C. Leemans, *Aegyptische hiëroglyphische lijkpapyrus, T. 3 van het Nederlandsche Museum van Oudheden te Leyden*, Leyden, 1882

The precise title of the Lady Taucherit is "Musician of Amun-Re, Singer of the Goddess Mut". In her lifetime she was one of the highest ranking women in Thebes.
Vignette of chapter 125 of the Book of the Dead.
As was stated in the captions to Plates 39—42, chapter 125 of the Book of the Dead is the one that is worked out in greatest detail, both in words and in pictures.
This illustration presents a scene of particular interest. The central figure is the god of wisdom, Thoth, who is painting the character of truth, or justice (Egyptian: Maat) in the manner of the Egyptian scribes and painters, using red and black paint. Behind him can be seen his writing tools — his pen-holder, his paint-bag, and his palette. This palette, like the oval one the god is holding, is prepared for black and red paint. Every Egyptian scribe and painter had these two colours on his palette.
In the lower register Horus can be seen busying himself at the scales. Normally the god of wisdom is also found near the scales. The division and sequence of the scenes differs from the normal scheme.
This Book of the Dead is among the most beautiful specimens of its kind left by the Ancient Egyptians. All passages of text are illustrated. The scroll is fully 12.5 metres long.

The god of wisdom Thoth kneeling papyrus, between 1085 and 950 BC

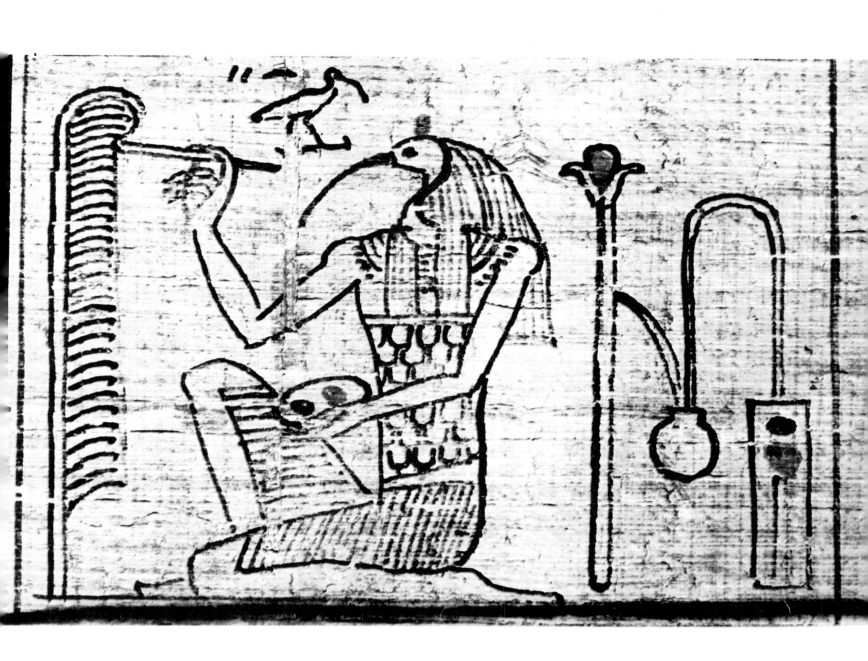

**49 The Book of the Dead
of the Lady Cheritwebeshet**
Twenty-first Dynasty
Cairo: Inv. No. 133
Papyrus A: H: 198 cm
W: 23.5 cm
Papyrus B: H: 119.1 cm
W: 23.5 cm

Published in: A. Piankoff, B. Rambova, *Egyptian Religious Texts and Representations*, vol. *III Mythological Papyri I/II*, New York, 1957
I p. 71, II Pap. No. 1

The killing of the Sun-god's enemies is one of the recurrent themes of certain genres of Other World literature. The form assumed by the Sun-god's chief enemy is generally that of the serpent Apophis. It is plainly the embodiment of evil and so it is not surprising that the killing of Apophis had an influence on the pharaoh's ritual duties. In Plate 49 the fire-spitting monster is being killed with a knife by a demon with an animal head. It is noteworthy that here, too, the thickening of various lines intensifies the impression of plasticity in the drawing.
Apophis was also killed by a spear (Plate 50). Only two gods accomplished this deed: the first was Seth, who was later proscribed and then became approximated to Apophis. Here he is seen with an animal head and spearing the serpent from the Sun-boat. Later this function passed to Osiris' son, Horus. This seems to be the point of contact where the accomplishments of Horus as son of Osiris meet those of the earthly pharaoh, who in theological terms is also Horus.
The originals of both these scenes are in Cairo. The papyrus is painted in black, red, white, green and brown.

**The killing of Apophis
papyrus, between 1085 and 950 BC**

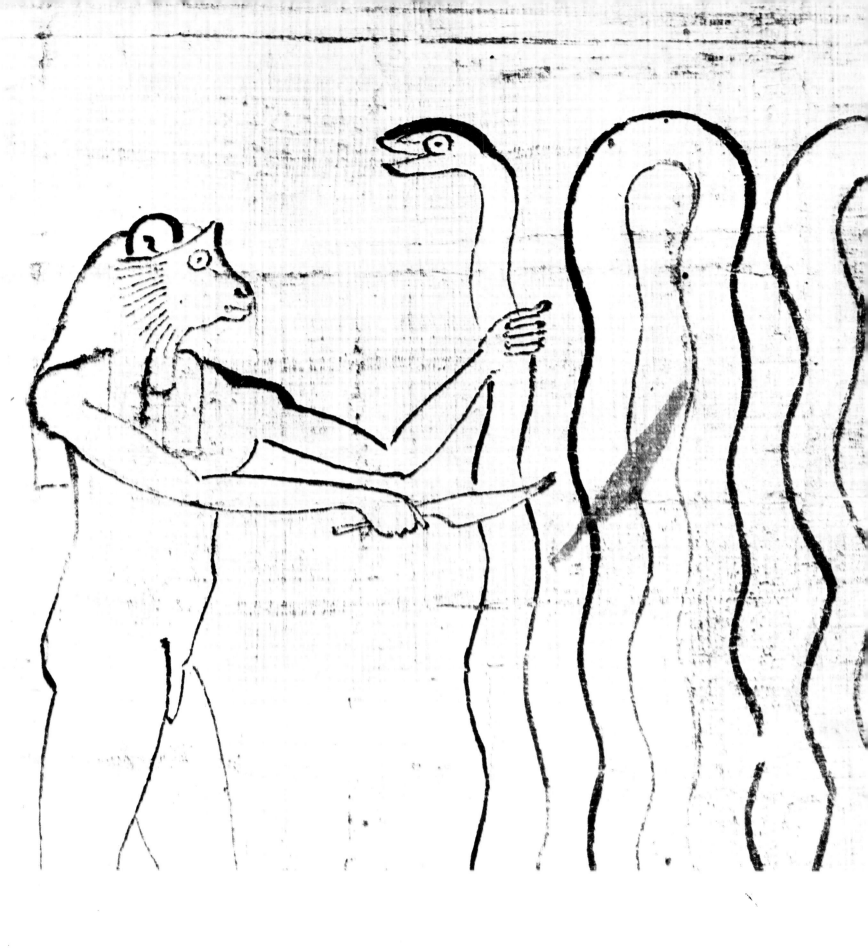

**50 The Book of the Dead
of the Lady Cheritwebeshet**
Twenty-first Dynasty
Cairo: Inv. No. 133
Papyrus A: H: 198 cm
W: 23.5 cm
Papyrus B: H: 119.1 cm
W: 23.5 cm

Explanatory text see Plate 49.

**The spearing of Apophis
papyrus, between 1085 and 950 BC**

51 Scene from a Guide to the Other World
Twentieth Dynasty (?)
Cairo

Guides to the Other World form a special category of literature on the Hereafter. Texts are generally deliberately omitted and instead certain symbols for the good and the evil parts of the Other World are taken over from themes in the Book of the Dead and are set forth one after the other.

This section shows, from right to left: a winged snake, the Guardian of the Realms of the Dead; Maat, the goddess of Justice; the Phoenix, as a symbol of reincarnation; the scarab, as bearer of similar hopes for the dead; and part of a heart, which symolizes the frequent exorcizing of the heart in the Book of the Dead. Here the empty section of the heart stands for content and function. The dead man (who is not visible here, since he is placed further to the right) is turning to the heart, entreating it not to speak out against him.

The life-cycle is here represented as an assembled group comprising a serpent, phoenix and beetle.

So far, eight specimens of this genre of Other World literature have been found and published, this one being the ninth. They probably represent a local Theban speciality.

**Scene from a Guide to the Other World
papyrus, probably between 1200 and 1085 BC**

52 The Book of the Dead
of the Lady Taucherit
Twenty-first Dynasty (from Thebes)
Nederlandsches Museum van Oudheden te Leyden: Cat.
Leemans T. 3

Published by C. Leemans, *Aegyptische hiëroglyphische lijk-papyrus, T. 3 van het Nederlandsche Museum van Oudheden te Leyden*, Leyden, 1882

Vignette of chapter 110 of the Book of the Dead.
"Beginning of the spells of the field of offerings and the coming-out by day."
The dead person, as previously stated, has to work in the Egyptian equivalent of the Elysian Fields (Iaru Field) in the Realm of the Blessed, apart from carrying on all the other functions of life.
In the top row the lady is praying to the various divinities who inhabit this Field of Offerings. The second row continues the description of adoration and sacrifices. On the left-hand side the edge of the field is visible and the Lady Taucherit can be seen bending down and gathering ears of corn into her little sack. In front of her men with sickles are harvesting the corn. The description of agricultural work in the Other World continues in the third row, with scenes of ploughing and sowing. The next row concludes this cycle of agricultural scenes. The last row, the staircase on the left, illustrates the second paragraph of chapter 110 in the Book of the Dead: "Spell for the descent to the judgment hall of Osiris and the veneration of the divinities who rule the Underworld. Of the going-in and the coming-out of the Underworld, for a sojourn in the Iaru Field, to be mighty there, to be blissful there, to plough there, to gather the harvest there, to eat there, to drink there, to be a husband (wife) there and to discharge all functions as on earth."
The Realm of the Blessed is girded by a broad stream of water. It separates the individual registers in a way that is graphically highly impressive.

Scenes in the Iaru Field
papyrus, between 1075 and 950 BC

**53 The Book of the Dead
of the Lady Taucherit**
Twenty-first Dynasty (from Thebes)
Nederlandsches Museum van Oudheden te Leyden: Cat.
Leemans T. 3

Published by C. Leemans, *Aegyptische hiëroglyphische lijk-papyrus, T. 3 van het Nederlandsche Museum van Oudheden te Leyden*, Leyden, 1882

Vignette of chapter 110 of the Book of the Dead.
The dead can also move about on the streams of water seen
in the picture. The very fine structure of the papyrus is
clearly seen in this specimen, though the ribbing must
have been an obstacle to the painter's brush; indeed,
breaks in the lines can be discerned here.
It was at this time that black paint was discovered for
graphic work on papyrus. This plate is a convincing example of this (cf. Plate 46).

**Scenes on the streams of water in the Iaru Field
papyrus, between 1075 and 950 BC**

54 Scenes from a Book of the Dead
Twentieth Dynasty
Cairo

The Cairo Book of the Dead serves as an example of work of very poor quality. We reproduce one section of it here. This work should be dated to the New Kingdom and the robes of the owner (not visible here) seem to confirm this. Several themes from scenes in the Book of the Dead are entered here one after the other, hastily and, it appears, sometimes without being understood. There is virtually no text, which shows that the sacred book was taken here to be an amulet. The original syntactical function of text and painted scenes in the Book of the Dead seems to have been distorted till it became merely a functional object, an amulet. The very possession of a papyrus with written characters and painted symbols, as well as divine figures, seems to have been a decisive factor.

**Scenes with Isis and Nephthys
papyrus, between 1200 and 1085 BC**

55 The Book of the Dead of Ta-nefer

Twenty-first Dynasty

Cairo

On this vignette of the Book of the Dead, Ta-nefer, the Third Prophet of Amon, is shown making sacrifices to Osiris. A table of offerings is loaded with bread, wine, meat and fruit and flowers. They are the climax of the scene and, like all the details in this section, are drawn with love. Ta-nefer is pouring libations with his right hand, while in his left he is holding a receptacle of the ritual burning of incense. The robes of the dead man and his shaven head are external symbols of his office.

Although the layout left ample space for writing, here, as in most papyri, the scribe seems to have been fighting a hopeless battle against the painter, who claimed far more space. He was the first to inscribe the papyrus, and was therefore at an advantage from the outset. The scribe who drew the characters then inscribed the space left to him with texts that were quite out of proportion. This means that text runs very closely to the painting and does not improve the overall visual impression created by the picture, as it does in Plate 56, the Book of the Dead of the Lady Cheritwebeshet.

In examining this drawing the first thing that strikes us is the dark colour scheme. The colours were originally far lighter and can be assumed to have changed. But an intense colour scheme such as that found to this day in the Book of the Dead of Kenna (Plate 37) seems unlikely for Ta-nefer's Book of the Dead. Other circumstances may have contributed to this. By that time, for instance, black must have been considered a colour (Plate IV: the Book of the Dead of the Lady Taucherit). The dots on the leopard's skin which are outlined in black and other details on the priest's robes give the figure a good deal of weight. How the painter achieved a visual balance between the priest and the heavily laden table of offerings cannot be ascertained today because of the state of the papyrus. He probably tried to give the table of offerings lightness by using very light shades of colour. The same applies to the treatment of the sacrificial loaves and the lotus flowers. The fingers curved in a Mannerist manner and the head with the elongated skull are characteristic aspects of Amarna art which were taken over into painting in the Ramesses period.

This picture documents the beginning of the "black and white" technique of the late period, while still containing elements of the style of the Ramesses period.

Sacrifice before Osiris
papyrus, between 1085 and 950 BC

**56 The Book of the Dead
of the Lady Cheritwebeshet**
Twenty-first Dynasty
Cairo: Inv. No. 133
Papyrus A: H: 198 cm
           W: 23.5 cm
Papyrus B: H: 119.1 cm
           W: 23.5 cm

Published in: A. Piankoff, B. Rambova, *Egyptian Religious Texts and Representations, vol. III Mythological Papyri I/II*, New York, 1957
I p. 71, II Pap. No. 1

Vignette of chapter 42 of the Book of the Dead.
This Book of the Dead of a high-ranking lady in Theban society can be taken as an outstanding specimen of the art of the late period. The text and vignettes, as the illustrations show, are in perfect harmony. One could say that the text forms a graphic accompaniment to the picture, as in Chinese pictorial inscriptions. The work was probably designed on the grand scale so as to encompass both pictures and text. The artist who painted the characters and the draughtsman seem to have worked with exceptional precision. The quality of the papyrus is a clue to the rank of the artists who covered it with words and pictures in their workshops. Such valuable work was certainly made for a client who occupied a high position in Egyptian society. As can be seen from the marginal notes to the first picture in the series in the Book of the Dead of Cheritwebeshet, this lady was a "Lady of the House, Chantress of Amon". Moreover, she held the official rank of "Second Prophet of the Great Mut", the wife of Amon, the chief god of Thebes.
The stress on sensuality of form and colour is striking in this papyrus. Let us begin with a description of the lady. She is kneeling on a line representing a bank and is drinking the fresh waters of the Other World. Her large wig of long plaits and curls is slightly untidy. Some strands of hair are falling forwards, while others slide sideways and a few are touching the water. This lively play of the hair conveys an impression of great lifelikeness, which is intensified by the delicate manner in which the artist has portrayed the female body. The full breasts are stressed by a dress belted in the Empire manner. The flowing lines marking abdomen and thighs contrast with the exaggeratedly long shins and finely shaped feet. Altogether the elongated limbs effectively contrast with the lady's full body and this contrast gives the picture an erotic impact. The kneeling position derives from a tradition in which the king is represented offering sacrifices to the gods. While in pictures of that kind the toes of both feet of the worshipping king are bent under and, as a rule, his left leg kneels in front while the right is stretched backward, here the

reverse is true. The act of kneeling down is shown clearly enough, but the artist, who must have the picture of the king at sacrifice in his mind's eye, changed the overall impression of the picture. The left leg is now stretched backward, while the right is in front. But this foot is moved in front of the left leg, although it ought not to be visible at all.
On the opposite side a crocodile is depicted in great detail. A sycamore symbolizes the freshness and pleasantness of the water, its leaves being made up of big, carefully arranged dots of paint.
The sequence of the scenes on the papyrus seems to be split up into units. The Egyptian sycamore, the band of writing, the kneeling lady and the crocodile form one unit. The dominant centre of the next scene is the young Sun-god, who is placed in the middle of an oval with his symbols of might and a child's hairstyle as proof of his youthfulness.
The serpent and the two arms that rise from it, the antelope head and the pride of lions, derive their symbolism from the New Kingdom guides to the Other World. We have no space here to explain each detail, but in the last analysis these symbols explain the dead person's desire to be born anew each day, as the Sun-god is. A baboon is greeting the rising sun.
In the depiction of the individual figures a certain solidity of body is evident, in spite of the elegance of the flowing lines.

**Dead lady drinking the fresh water
of the Other World
papyrus, between 1085 and 950 BC**

**57 The Book of the Dead
of the Lady Cheritwebeshet**
Twenty-first Dynasty
Cairo: Inv. No. 133
Papyrus A: H: 198 cm
    W: 23.5 cm
Papyrus B: H: 119.1 cm
    W: 23.5 cm

Published in: A. Piankoff, B. Rambova, *Egyptian Religious Texts and Representations, vol. III Mythological Papyri I/II*, New York, 1957
I p. 71, II Pap. No. 1

Vignette of chapter 63 of the Book of the Dead.
The content of this scene is clear in its significance. The dead woman is being drenched with jugs of holy water. This water pours "life and well-being" over the dead person. These two elements are expressed in the corresponding hieroglyphs for life and well-being. The hieroglyphs seem to run in a long chain from one of the sacrificial jugs. The drenching of the dead person with holy water is usually a priest's function. In this case, the dead woman being a member of the royal family, it is done by Horus and Thoth.
The dead lady is again depicted to perfection. Her face bears marks of portraiture. The treatment of the upper left arm is striking. Some strands of the luxurious wig are falling onto it and the painter has tried to achieve the effect of a veil. The contours of the shoulder and the upper arm are clearly distinguishable but their colours are subdued.

Purification
papyrus, between 1085 and 950 BC

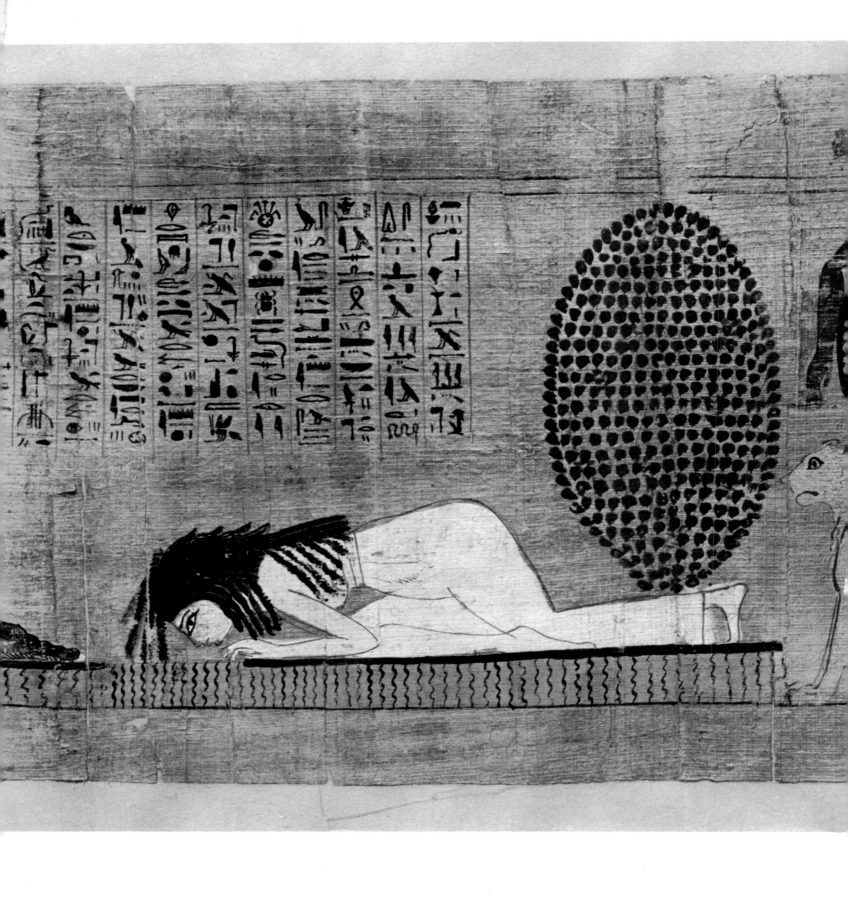

**58 The Book of the Dead
of the Lady Cheritwebeshet**
Twenty-first Dynasty
Cairo: Inv. No. 133
Papyrus A: H: 198 cm
            W: 23.5 cm
Papyrus B: H: 119.1 cm
            W: 23.5 cm

Published in: A. Piankoff, B. Rambova, *Egyptian Religious
Texts and Representations, vol. III Mythological Papyri
I/II*, New York, 1957
I p. 71, II Pap. No. 1

Vignette of chapter 110 of the Book of the Dead.
The scenes of labour in the fields, ploughing, sowing and
harvesting, have been discussed on a different occasion
(cf. Plate 52). A striking feature here, as in the other two
scenes, is the revelation of details and the feeling of lifelikeness. A point of detail worth noting is that while working the lady has pushed her wig to the back of her head.
The seeds she is broadcasting can almost be touched, in
accordance with the trend towards realistic depiction.
The geography of the Other World is again indicated by
the thick line of the ploughed field and the water running
vertically below it. It is surprising that this region of the
Other World is conceived as a hilly one. In this sector the
painter's work appears to be slightly crude and he has not
followed the contours drawn by the draughtsman. The
face and the body of the lady assume their proper meaning
thanks to the far more skilful fingers of the contour painter,
who in following the main painter completed the latter's
work by giving the figures red contour lines.

**Scenes in the Iaru Field
papyrus, between 1085 and 950 BC**

**59 The Book of the Dead
of the Lady Cheritwebeshet**
Twenty-first Dynasty
Cairo: Inv. No. 133
Papyrus A: H: 198 cm
           W: 23.5 cm
Papyrus B: H: 119.1 cm
           W: 23.5 cm

Published in: A. Piankoff, B. Rambova, *Egyptian Religious Texts and Representations, vol. III Mythological Papyri I/II*, New York, 1957
I p. 71, II Pap. No. 1

The dead woman is standing with arms raised in front of the barge of the Sun-god, praying. In the picture can be seen jackals and Uraea with human arms drawing the barge. The reason for her prayers is repeated in the text:
"Worship of Re-Harachte, the great God, Lord of the Skies, by the righteous Cheritwebeshet."
The layout of the composition is again very strict. The lady on the right-hand side is counter-balanced by rows of deities. The upper row, in particular, reveals the specifically Egyptian principle of building up on one plane. The jackals are standing side by side, each slightly overlapping his neighbour and appearing to stand behind him. The resulting overlapping is relieved by the use of lighter shades of colour, so that all the limbs are clearly visible, even those covered by the overlapping parts.
The treatment of the lower row is less complicated. Here overlapping would have involved a loss of the visual impact. The Uraea, again sitting in a row, are projected onto the plane individually.
The height of this picture is determined by the height of the lady at her prayers. The position of the script is less successful in this vignette. We are aware of the lack of space, especially in the middle column. Two of the hieroglyphs are slightly out of line so as not to collide with the right hand of the worshipping lady. The arm movement and the gracefully inclined body corresponding to the line that links the jackals prove that the painter possessed great skill, for he created lines of tension across the picture with the aid of such lines. This is even clearer in the lower section of the picture, where the Uraea again seem to be linked together. They are set deeper back in the picture and the swaying line of their bodies is repeated in the lady's swaying robes.

**Dead lady at prayers
papyrus, between 1085 and 950 BC**

60 The Book of the Dead of Djoser, Priest of the Goddess of Love Bastet

Ptolemaic Period
Cairo (from Saqquara)

Vignette of Chapter 125 of the Book of the Dead.

Osiris is seated in majesty in front of a table laden with gift offerings. He is enclosed in a shrine and is depicted in his standard form as a mummy, with his insignia as "Ruler of the West". A band of inscription gives his name and title. Above the two pictures there is a row of mummified deities adorned with the feathers of Maat (justice), who are Osiris' assessors in the Court of Judgment. They are sitting in the background and are consequently assigned to a line in the upper part of the picture. The dead man is making a sacrifice to them, too, and has set up a table of offerings. The scene is set in the Hall of Osiris, to which the dead have to descend.

In scenes of this type the room can usually be recognized from its architectural elements. Most frequently, as is the case here, these consist of lotus columns supporting a heavy, richly decorated roof.

This papyrus is a typical product of its time. The delicate treatment of the lines and the vivid colouring are proof of great craftsmanship, which must have been formed by methodical training aimed at protecting the Egyptian manner of art from the impact of the Greek spirit. The reliance on the style of the Old and the Middle Kingdoms can be clearly felt. It was there that artists studied form and from there that they copied it. The result is a work of truly perfect craftsmanship. Yet such works lack aesthetic impact. The movements in this case are rather stiff and correspond, together with the symmetrical layout of the picture, to an external strength in the manner of expression.

Judgment scene and Hall of Osiris papyrus, between 305 and 30 BC

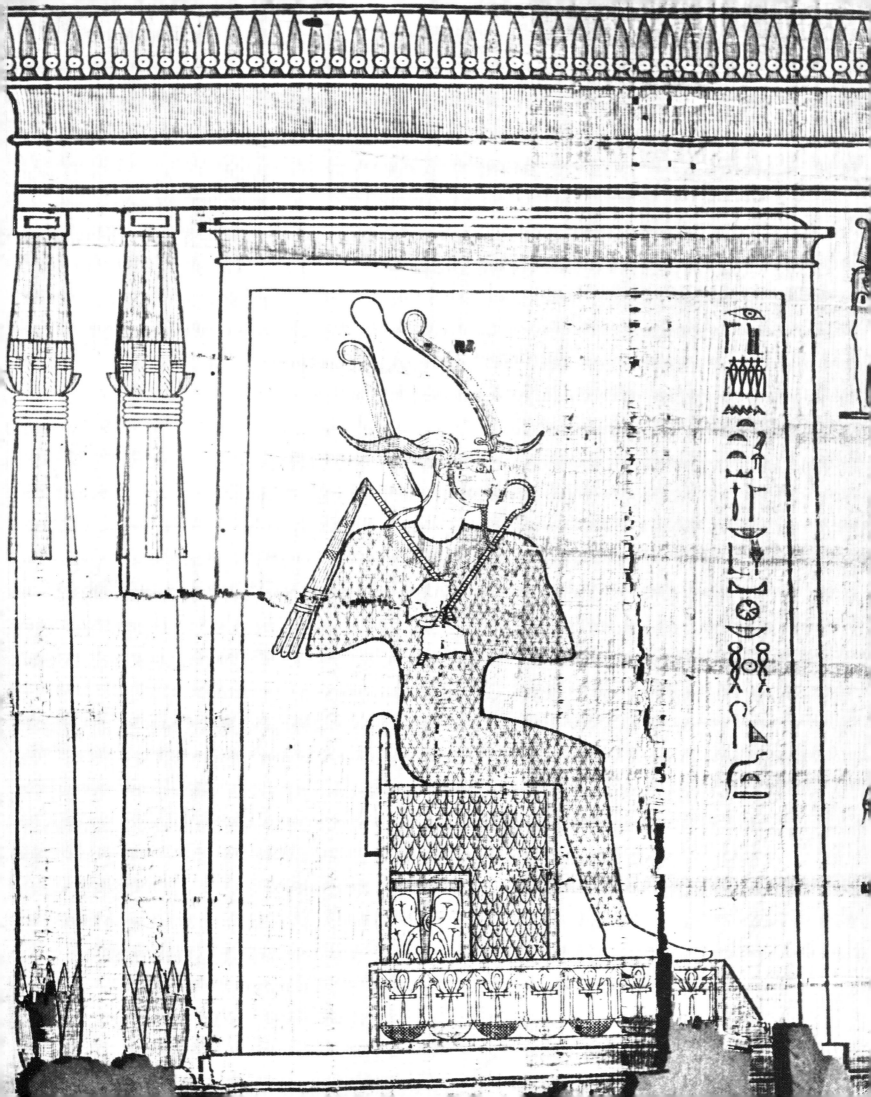

61 Scene from a Book of the Dead
Ptolemaic Period (?)

Vignette of chapter 125 of the Book of the Dead.
This fragment depicts a scene with the scales and the
table of offerings in the presence of Osiris, with the god
of Wisdom, Thoth, standing in the rear. The delicacy
both of the papyrus and of the drawing should be noted.

Judgment scene before Osiris
papyrus, between 305 and 30 BC

B